FALKIRK CO
30124
D1100655
FALKIRK LIBRARY
STREET
FK FK1 5AU
03605

DRESSMAKING
200 QUESTIONS ANSWERED

DRESSMAKING
200 QUESTIONS ANSWERED

Questions answered on everything
from stitching seams to setting in sleeves

Mary McCarthy

Search Press

A Quantum Book

Published in 2012 by Search Press Ltd.
Wellwood, North Farm Road,
Tunbridge Wells,
Kent TN2 3DR

This book is produced by
Quantum Publishing
6 Blundell Street
London
N7 9BH

Copyright © 2012 Quantum Publishing

All rights reserved. This book is protected by copyright.
No part of it may be reproduced, stored in a retrieval system,
or transmitted in any form or by any other means,
without the prior permission in writing of the Publisher,
nor be otherwise circulated in any form of binding or
cover other than that in which it is published and
without a similar condition including this condition being
imposed on the subsequent publisher.

ISBN: 978-1-84448-839-1

QUM2QAD

Publisher: Sarah Bloxham
Managing Editor: Jennifer Eiss
Editor: Caroline Smith
Project Editor: Samantha Warrington
Assistant Editor: Jo Morley
Design: Dave Jones
Photographer: Marcos Bevilacqua
Production Manager: Rohana Yusof

Printed in China by Midas Printing International Ltd.

CONTENTS

Falkirk Council	
FK	
Askews & Holts	
646.404	£9.99

INTRODUCTION

Sewing has been my passion from a very young age. I remember watching attentively as my grandmother and older sister cut and stitched pieces of fabric together to create an original garment. How exciting! At the age of eight, I made a pair of blue-and-brown striped shorts, and from then on, I was completely hooked.

My passion was encouraged by my parents – my mother with her sense of style, and my father, who promised to buy me as much fabric as I wished, as long as I used it to practise my new-found hobby. I enrolled in numerous sewing classes and spent most of my free time at the sewing machine.

Over the years, my enthusiasm for all things related to fabric and fashion did not wane. I earned a B.S. in Fashion Merchandising and began a career in retailing and business management. I enjoyed travel opportunities and learned many skills, but I longed to get back to what I loved most – sewing. After many years in corporate life, I took the plunge and started a custom dressmaking business, specialising in bridal and formal wear. Sewing for others allowed me to work on a broad range of fabrics, designs and body types to meet the needs and desires of my clients. I developed my skills and discovered new techniques that built on my formal training. My goal has always been to find the most practical and efficient approach to complete a task, without compromising the quality of the work.

I am also passionate about sharing what I know with others. Currently I teach a variety of skill levels, including pre-teens, college design students, and adults. Nothing instills in you the details of a technique like having to demonstrate and explain it to someone else. My students challenge me daily to find a better way to describe a technique or solve a sewing problem. To them, I owe many thanks for helping me move forward on my own sewing journey. I'm also grateful to my needlecraft mentors and colleagues, who encourage me with their enthusiasm and guidance with whatever project I am working on.

I urge you to get together with other sewing enthusiasts on a regular basis. You learn so much as you share ideas and admire one another's accomplishments and finished projects! The process of sewing should be as enjoyable as the end result.

If you are a beginner, then this book will guide you through the most basic tasks, from what tools you need through to sewing on a button. If you have already spent many hours at the sewing machine, you will find new ways to add to your own favourite techniques, as well as benefiting from more advanced topics.

Whatever your present skill level, I hope this book inspires and encourages you to be creative, try new things, and most importantly, have fun.

Keep Sewing!

Mary

When you are making your own clothes, you will make the decision as to whether you want your stitching to be visible – and form a decorative feature – or invisible. If you want to do decorative stitching then you can use a contrasting coloured thread but, generally speaking, you will want to use a thread that matches your fabric. However, to ensure that the the stitching shown in some of the pictures in this book is easy to see, the sewing has been done with a strongly coloured thread, instead of a matching one.

1

SEWING EQUIPMENT

Question 1:
What tools do I need to get started?

Now that you have decided to embark on your sewing journey, you will need to invest in a few basic tools, including a sewing machine. If you are going to purchase a new one, look for these essential functions: straight and zigzag stitch, a backstitch (or reverse) function, a buttonhole maker and a few decorative stitches.

The machine should create smooth, even stitches, on several different types of fabric. It should also come with a few accessories or attachments and an instruction manual. Prices range from under £100 to several thousand pounds for brand new ones, so before you buy, consider your skill level and how often you plan to sew. Purchasing a sewing machine is a bit like buying a car – ideally you should 'test drive' several models before making a final decision. Machines can be found at large fabric stores and haberdashers. If you are planning on buying a top-of-the-range model, it is a good idea to buy from a dealer who can also service the machine if needed.

Other tools you will need to get started include suitable scissors, a seam ripper, tape measure, seam gauge, tailor's chalk or marking pencil, pins and a pin cushion, and hand-sewing needles.

Last but not least, you will need a good working iron and ironing board. Pressing as you sew is essential to achieving good results. So if you are not familiar with pressing techniques, you will learn quickly how valuable this step is.

EXPERT TIP

❝ **Essential items are often sold together as part of a basic sewing kit. This is an economical way to get started but you will probably want to upgrade your tools as you get more sewing experience.** ❞

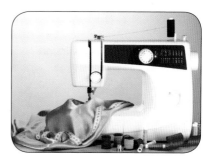

ABOVE A good quality sewing machine is an essential when dressmaking.

Question 2:
What kinds of needles and pins do I need?

Throughout the sewing process, you will need both hand and sewing machine needles, straight pins and, occasionally, safety pins. All pins and needles should be rustproof with a sharp point.

• Hand needles
These come in a variety of sizes and lengths. For general purposes, choose a pack of sharps, which are medium length and will work for most of your hand sewing. Smaller needles are available for working with sheer, fine fabrics and larger ones are available for working on thicker fabrics as well as for sewing on buttons (larger needles are also easier to hold).

• Sewing machine needles
These also come in a variety of sizes ranging from size 60/8 to 100/19. Choose the size according to the type of fabric you are working with. Most fabrics work well with a universal needle, size 75/11 or 80/12. The larger sizes are used for stitching several layers or thicker fabrics such as denim. Smaller sizes should be used for stitching sheers, silk, and other lightweight fabrics.

Knit fabrics require a ballpoint needle. Consult your owner's manual for what specific type of needles to use in your sewing machine. Other types of speciality needles exist for use on leather and water repellent fabrics.

• Pins
These should be sharp and easy to handle, because you will be using pins every time you sew. The best choice should measure at least 2.5cm (1in) long and slide easily in and out of your fabric. Glass-head pins are a great choice because they are sharp, a little longer than those found in sewing kits, and will not melt if your iron touches the glass head. They are more expensive, but it's well worth spending extra on such an essential tool.

EXPERT TIP

66 To avoid snags or puckers in your seams, change your sewing machine needle after completing each project, or at least after several hours of sewing. 99

Question 3:
What kind of sewing machine accessories do I need?

All sewing machines come with a small kit or a packet of accessories or attachments. Generally speaking this includes a standard or all-purpose presser foot, a zip foot, a buttonhole attachment foot, bobbins and/or a bobbin case, and a seam ripper. You may also get some suitable sewing-machine oil and a small cleaning brush.

Other optional feet that may be included are a cording foot, rolled hemmer, blind stitch or darning foot. Your owner's manual will guide you through the process of inserting and using them properly. Optional feet and attachments that can be purchased separately may include an invisible zip foot, darning foot, narrow rolled hemmer, or blind hemmer. The invisible zip foot is used when you want to insert an invisible zip (see Question 188). Most of your basic sewing tasks, however, can be done with your all-purpose foot.

Question 4:
What type of cutting tools do I need?

Good, sharp scissors are one of your most important tools. Choose a pair of dressmaking or bent-handled shears. The blades should be at least 18cm (7in) long with handles that fit comfortably around your four fingers and thumb. Bent shears rest flat on the cutting surface to ensure accuracy and smooth, even cutting strokes. These scissors should not be used for any other purpose but to cut fabric; otherwise, the shears quickly become dull and will no longer cut sharp edges on your fabric. You also need another pair of scissors for cutting paper (such as pattern pieces) and materials other than fabric. Pinking shears, which have a 'zigzag' edge, help reduce fraying along the raw edge of seams. These are useful if you do not own an overlocker (see Question 17).

A small pair of scissors with a 5–10cm (2–4in) blade, such as embroidery scissors, are also handy to keep near your sewing machine for cutting threads and smaller areas as you assemble your garment; for example, clipping curves or trimming corners. A rotary cutter (which looks like a pizza cutter) cuts through several layers of fabric accurately and easily, but requires a cutting mat on which to work. It is often used to cut straight lines against a clear ruler, but it's also a wonderful tool for cutting slippery fabrics (such as silk) because it does so precisely and with no lifting of the fabric off the cutting surface. Finally, a seam ripper is the smallest of your essential cutting tools, but likely to be your most valuable – it removes sewn stitches when you need to correct an error. It's sometimes called a 'reverse' stitcher.

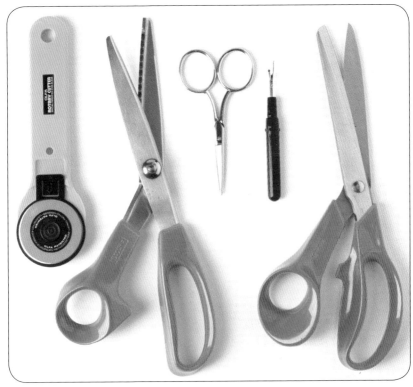

ABOVE The most useful cutting tools for dressmaking are (from left to right) a rotary cutter; pinking shears; embroidery scissors; a seam ripper, and dressmaking shears.

Question 5:
How do I choose the correct thread?

The type of thread you use should correspond with your fabric choice; see the chart below as a guide to thread types.

You may see other varieties of thread on the market – labelled as hand-sewing thread or heavy quilting thread, for example – but all-purpose thread will do the job just as well. Be sure to read the labels carefully on the end of the thread spools before you make your final choice.

EXPERT TIP

66 If you are trying to match thread colours to fabric, and find yourself stuck between a lighter and a darker shade, opt for the darker shade – it will blend in better with the fabric. Lighter shades tend to catch light and show more against a dark fabric. 99

Thread	Fabric Type
All purpose	Polyester, synthetic, natural, or blends; knit and woven fabrics
Cotton	Natural fibres (cotton, bamboo); light to medium weight fabrics
Cotton-covered polyester	Denim; medium weight fabrics
Nylon	Upholstery; interior furnishings
Silk	Silk; wool; hand sewing; decorative stitches
Rayon/rayon blend	Decorative or machine embroidery sewing

Question 6:
What type of iron do I need for the best results?

You do not need an expensive iron to achieve good results, but you do need to have an iron on hand while you sew. A garment that is pressed throughout the sewing process can mean the difference between a professional-looking garment and one that shouts 'home-made'!

Irons vary widely and the amount of sewing you plan to do will determine your choice. Most irons have a steam feature and an automatic shut-off option (the iron turns off after a period of time if unused). This is a good safety feature, but you need to consider how convenient it will be for you to continually wait after a long pause for the iron to reheat. Some irons designed for sewing have a longer shut-off time, such as 30 minutes (before it shuts off). Others have no shut off at all and are designed with separate water tanks that allow for more steam to generate before having to refill them.

Question 7:
I've heard of a press cloth; what is it for?

A press cloth is a must-have at your ironing board for two important reasons. It helps prevent scorching on delicate fabrics, and it is used when you apply fusible interfacing to small garment pieces such as collar and cuffs. It must be made of a natural fibre such as cotton; a large handkerchief works well, or make your own out of a sheer natural fibre such as silk organza. This type of silk is durable enough to prevent scorching and, because it is sheer, it allows you to see your work as you press. Press cloths can be purchased at a fabric store, but if you make your own cut a large square of fabric and label one side 'this side up'. This will keep sticky residue from transferring accidentally to the next project.

Question 8:
Do I need a tailor's ham?

You probably do not need to invest in a tailor's ham right away, but it is a useful tool for pressing along curved areas such as darts and seams. A ham is oval shaped, about the size of a rugby football, and stuffed tightly with sawdust. The sawdust absorbs steam as you apply your iron to your garment placed over the ham.

The cover is made of cotton and wool, which also absorb steam as you press. The curves of the ham replicate the form of the body, allowing you to create shape in your garment as you press along seams and darts. The ham is placed under the garment while you steam and press the area. The shape of the ham creates shape in the garment.

Question 9:
What are a clapper and a point press, and how do I use them?

These are both additional pressing tools that help make your garment look professionally sewn and finished. The number of pressing tools available is a clear indication of the importance of of this task in dressmaking!

A clapper has several different shapes combined into one tool to help press different areas of your garment. The wide surface (about 10cm (4in) across) helps put sharp creases in hems and other folds. The thin side (about 12mm (½in) across) flattens seams, and the point at one end (the 'point press' part of the tool) allows you to press the corners in cuffs and collars. Because it is made of wood, steam is absorbed into the clapper as you apply steam and pressure to the various surfaces.

Question 10:
What are a sleeve board and a sleeve roll, and how do I use them?

A sleeve board and sleeve roll, two more great pressing tools, are designed to make your sleeves look well tailored and professional. The sleeve board is like a mini-ironing board with a soft cover over a hard surface. The narrow shape fits easily into a sleeve that is already sewn together so you can press the seam flat. Turn the sleeve inside out to access the seam and slide it over the small end before you apply steam and pressure with your iron.

A sleeve roll looks like a large sausage (about 25cm (10in) long) and is stuffed with sawdust, like the tailor's ham. It also has a cover made of wool and cotton fabric. This can also be used to press sewn-up sleeves by inserting it inside them before you steam and press. A sleeve roll also makes a great tool for pressing any type of seam open and flat. Because the surface is curved, the edges of a seam will not show through as you press.

ABOVE A sleeve board looks like a very small ironing board. Once erected on its built-in stand, the sleeve board can be used on a table top or on the ironing board.

Question 11:
What marking tools do I need?

Every sewing box should include fabric marking tools. There are several types available including tailor's chalk, fabric pens, and tracing paper and wheel.

Sewing patterns have several lines and symbols printed on the tissue pieces that must be transferred to the fabric after it's been cut out and before you start to sew. Some of the most common markings to transfer include darts, pleats, tucks, collar points, buttonholes, and pockets. Tailor's chalk comes in several forms – pencil, wheel, and square – and is likely the one you will use the most. Fabric pens may be water-soluble and rinse away when the garment is machine washed or rinsed out by hand. They can also fade in humid weather. Air-soluble pens disappear after 12 or more hours. This can be tricky if you wait to begin sewing your project – you may find the markings have disappeared!

ABOVE You can use a wheel and special chalk-impregnated paper to transfer pattern markings to your fabric.

Question 12:
How do I use tailor's chalk?

Tailor's chalk is a popular marking tool because it can be used in almost all situations that require you to transfer markings from pattern to fabric. It comes in several colours and when picking a chalk to use you should opt for one that contrasts with your fabric (yellow and blue chalks are very useful). Tailor's chalk is available in flat pieces, or in a crayon format.

To mark a dot, for example, place a pin through all layers of fabric and pattern, then peel back each layer, and place a chalk mark where the pin pierces each layer of fabric. Be sure to mark on the wrong side of the fabric. Repeat this for as many dots as needed on, say, a dart or pleat line.

ABOVE Pierce pattern markings with a pin and then peel back the pattern and first layer of fabric. Use tailor's chalk to mark the pin's position.

Question 13:
How do I use carbon tracing paper?

Carbon tracing paper is coated with coloured chalk and washes or rubs out of most fabrics easily. That said, it is advisable to do a test on a scrap of your fabric first.

The paper is sandwiched between the pattern piece and the fabric after cutting out with the chalk touching the wrong side of the garment pieces. The wheel is then traced along the lines and symbols you wish to transfer. When you remove the pattern pieces and the paper, chalk marks will appear on the fabric where you need to sew or match symbols and other marks. The wheel is a useful tool to have, as it will last a long time, and is an accurate way to mark your pattern pieces.

ABOVE Slip carbon tracing paper between your pattern and the fabric (wrong side up) and trace the wheel across features such as darts in order to transfer the markings.

Question 14:
How do I use a tape measure?

A tape measure is the primary tool needed to take body measurements, but you will also find it essential to measure pattern pieces, garment lengths and widths, and many other elements in the sewing process. A tape measure is at least 150cm (60in) long and is marked with centimetres on one side, and feet and inches on the other.

The ends of a good quality tape measure are bound with lightweight metal or plastic, which helps with accuracy and durability. The tape should be made of plastic that will not stretch when pulled snugly. All basic sewing kits will include a tape measure since you always need one readily to hand when sewing.

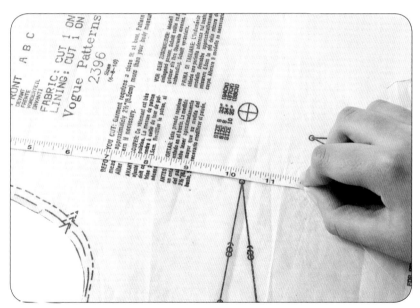

ABOVE You can use a tape measure to gather essential information about your pattern, such as the distance between the marked bust point and the shoulder.

Question 15:
What is a seam gauge?

A seam gauge is a small ruler used to measure areas that are 10cm (4in) or smaller. It features a separate slider that moves up and down the centre of the ruler to mark a specific measurement. For example, you can use it to ensure buttonholes are spaced evenly at, say, 5cm (2in) apart. All you need to do is move the slider to the 5cm (2in) mark on the ruler where it will stay in place, and then use this as you mark the position of each buttonhole.

You can also use a seam gauge to check parts of a garment that should match after sewing. For instance, the placement of identical patch pockets, or the width of a hem allowance around an entire hemmed edge.

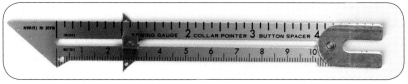

ABOVE A seam gauge is a small but very useful measuring tool for any sewing box.

Question 16:
What kind of rulers do I need?

Rulers are an essential sewing tool. They can be used for taking measurements and for drawing lines when you are working with your fabric and/or the sewing pattern laid out on a flat surface.

The length of a metre ruler (or yardstick) makes it useful for measuring the length and width of fabric or pattern pieces. It also helps you measure a hem if you try a garment on.

Clear, plastic rulers are usually considered a quilting tool but because they are transparent and have grid lines printed on the surface, they are very useful for garment sewing as well. They come in a variety of sizes from 30–90cm (12–36in) long.

A curved ruler or French curve is handy because it allows you to measure or draw lines that match body curves. I use both of these to redraw lines on a pattern when I make adjustments. I also use them to measure and mark lengths and curves on fabric.

Question 17:
What is an overlocker?

An overlocker (or a serger) looks slightly different from a sewing machine. It can hold up to five spools of thread (known as cone thread) and has two loopers instead of a bobbin to create a stitch. Unlike a sewing machine, an overlocker can sew a seam, finish the raw edge, and trim the excess seam allowance all in one step. It can also be used after you have stitched a seam on the sewing machine, to finish the raw edge and trim off the excess.

An overlocker is a wonderful tool, but it is not essential to have one. Most people invest in one only after acquiring good, basic sewing skills and are ready to take their sewing to the next level. You can finish and trim your seams by other satisfactory methods if you are not ready to acquire an overlockerr.

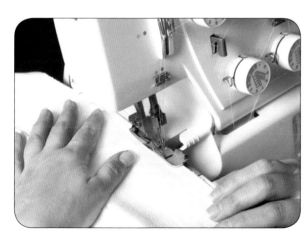

LEFT Although you may use an overlocker very much like a sewing machine, it differs in that it stitches, finishes and trims a seam in one operation.

MEASUREMENTS
AND FITTING

Question 18:
What body measurements do I need to take?

Accurate body measurements are a key element to creating a garment that fits well and feels comfortable. A good fit is also much more flattering than a bad one, no matter what your size or figure type.

To start, you need to take certain measurements to help you select the correct size pattern; these are your bust, high bust, waist, hip, and back-neck to waist measurements. See Question 19 on how to take accurate measurements. Once you've taken them you can match them to the correct pattern size on the back of the pattern envelope.

When you come to fine-tune the fit of your pattern you will need to take some additional body measurements. These are waist to floor, back width, shoulder to shoulder, shoulder width, front shoulder to bust point, arm circumference, and arm length. You will need these to make alterations to the pattern so the finished garment will fit your body shape.

It's advisable to keep a note of all these measurements; take a photocopy of the chart here and fill in the measurements as you take them. It's a good idea to update the measurements regularly and since these may change, complete the chart in pencil.

Measurement position	Your measurement
Bust	
Upper chest	
Waist	
Hips	
Back-neck to waist	
Waist to floor	
Back width	
Shoulder to shoulder	
Shoulder width	
Front shoulder to bust point	
Arm circumference	
Arm length	

EXPERT TIP

❝ Pattern sizes are generally larger than shop-bought clothes sizes, so don't worry if the correct size pattern seems big compared with your clothes' size. For example, you may wear a size 12, shop-bought skirt but require a size 14 or 16 pattern. ❞

Question 19:
How do I take accurate body measurements?

It will be much easier to take some of these measurements with the assistance of someone else, so ask for help in advance. Wear good fitting underwear rather than outer clothing as you will be more likely to get an accurate measurement.

As you take measurements and wrap the tape measure around your body, hold it with each thumb and forefinger. The tape should be snug around the area being measured, but not pinching. Record your findings on your measurement chart to the nearest centimetre (or half inch).

- **Bust**: this is taken around the fullest part of the bust.
- **Upper chest**: take this right under the arms and just above the bust.
- **Waist**: this is taken around your middle at, or just above your belly button. (See Question 35 for finding your natural waist.)
- **Hips**: the tape measure should be around the fullest part of your backside, 18–23cm (7–9in) below your waist.
- **Back-neck to waist**: get a friend to hold the end of the tape measure at the base of your neck

and measure down your back to your waist.
- **Waist to floor**: this is taken from the back waistline to the heel. Extra for shoes can be added later.
- **Back width**: getting a friend to help you, measure from under one arm to the other, across your back.
- **Shoulder to shoulder**: measure from the top of your left arm, where it meets the shoulder, across your back to the top of your right arm. You will need assistance with this one.
- **Shoulder width**: measure from the top of your arm to the base of your neck, along the shoulder.
- **Front shoulder to bust point**: find the centre point along the shoulder and measure down from here to the point of the bust.
- **Arm circumference**: the measurement should be taken around the fullest part of your upper arm, you may need a friend to help you take this one.
- **Arm length**: hold your arm slightly bent at the elbow and measure from the top of your arm, over your bent elbow and down to the wrist bone.

Question 20:
How do I know which size pattern to use?

All patterns have a size chart printed on the back of the envelope featuring three basic measurements: bust, waist, hip. The size charts are standard for all the major pattern companies, which means the measurements in any given size are the same, no matter what pattern company you choose. For example, the bust in a size-12 McCalls' pattern is the same as the bust in a Vogue. Once you decide on the correct pattern size (see Question 21) you can choose the same size in another pattern company.

However, there is one exception to this and it is in regard to bust size; if your bust measurement is more than 6.5cm (2½in) greater than your upper chest measurement, you should match your upper chest measurement (also known as high bust measurement) to the bust size on the pattern chart. This is because sewing patterns are all drafted to a B cup and if you exceed that cup size it is easier to make adjustments to the bust of a pattern rather than having to adjust a pattern that will be too big in the shoulder, upper chest, and neckline.

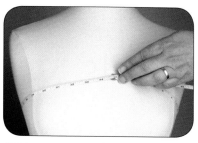

ABOVE Your upper chest measurement is taken above the bust line.

Question 21:
What if my measurements don't match the size chart?

When you take your measurements (bust, waist, and hip) to choose the right size pattern, they might not match up perfectly with each measurement in a given size, or they may match different sizes. For example, you may have a size 12 bust and a size 16 hip measurement. So which do you choose? The answer depends very much on what type of garment you are making. If it's a dress or top, choose the pattern that matches your bust or upper chest measurement (see Question 20); it's easier to add room to the hips on a dress pattern than reduce the pattern at the bust. If you are making a skirt or trousers, choose the size that matches your hip measurement. That is all you need to compare to buy the correct pattern.

EXPERT TIP

66 Patterns usually contain more than one size within a pattern envelope. This is especially helpful if you are making a dress and your bust is, say, a size 12, but your hips are a size 16: when you cut out the pattern tissue pieces, cut along the size 12 lines above the waist and flare out to the size 16 lines below the waist. 99

Question 22:
How do I choose a pattern for my skill level?

If you are new to sewing, it's a good idea to start out with something simple. Ideally, look for garments that have just two or three main pattern pieces, such as a front, back and sleeve; you should avoid patterns where the main part of the garment is made up of several different pieces.

If the pattern you like includes several other smaller pieces, such as pockets or ruffles, don't be put off. You can omit these details if you are not comfortable making them or if you want a simpler pattern than that shown on the envelope.

EXPERT TIP

66 Some of the companies that make sewing patterns manufacture a range of designs that are intended to be easier: look for those labelled 'easy' or 'simple'. You may also find some free patterns for beginners online; these can be downloaded to your home computer and then printed out. 99

Question 23:
How do I choose a pattern that will flatter me?

Most people's bodies fall into one of four types. These are the triangle, the inverted triangle, the rectangle, and the hourglass. If you are a triangle, then you will have a small bust and shoulders, and fuller hips and thighs; if you are an inverted triangle then you will be fuller at the bust and shoulders and narrow at the hips. Rectangle types are full at the waist and balanced between shoulder and hips. The hourglass has balanced shoulders and hips but a nipped-in waist. Clothing styles that suit one body type will not necessarily suit another.

EXPERT TIP

66 Fabric colours and patterns also play a part in how flattering a garment looks. Bright colours and large designs will emphasise any area of the body on which they are used, so take this into consideration. The same goes for dark, muted colours and smaller pattern motifs, which will have a minimising effect. 99

• Triangle
CHOOSE wide collars and necklines; gathers and yokes above the waist; a high waist or A-line silhouette.
AVOID detailed pockets at the hipline; raglan sleeves; gathered cuffs and wrists.

• Inverted triangle
CHOOSE patterns for garments with pocket details, and gathers or pleats at the hip; styles with minimal detail at the bust and shoulders.
AVOID high waistlines; wide collars; gathered sleeves.

• Rectangle
CHOOSE any pattern that features details which draw attention upward, such as yokes and gathers.
AVOID styles with details at the waist, such as contrasting belts, gathers and scarves.

• Hourglass
CHOOSE patterns with vertical lines, such as princess seams; styles that are belted at the waist.
AVOID large patterns; 'boxy' styles; any garment styles that are too full at the waist.

Question 24:
Should I make a practice garment before cutting the fabric?

Yes, this is a good idea, especially if you are new to the process of fitting a garment successfully. It is also a good idea if you are planning to use an expensive fabric or create a garment for a special occasion, such as a wedding gown. A practice garment is sometimes called a muslin or a toile because it is made out of muslin or other lightweight cotton fabric.

The toile is cut and sewn together for a test fitting. You can then make additional changes to the fit and style if needed. Once you are satisfied with the toile, you can transfer the changes back to your paper pattern, or you can even separate the toile pieces (i.e. take the practice garment apart) and use it as your final pattern. This may seem like an unnecessary extra step, but it is worthwhile in order

to avoid mistakes later on. Some changes have to be made at the cutting out stage, because it may be too late once you have cut out the garment in fabric!

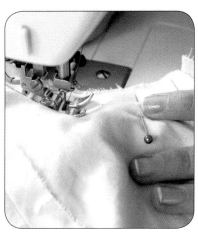

ABOVE A toile is usually made out of a cheap fabric such as calico. You can either hand tack or machine stitch the pieces together.

EXPERT TIP

❝ You need only to cut out and sew together the larger pieces of your test garment. Don't worry about stitching up the smaller pieces, such as the collar, pockets, facings or even the lining. ❞

Question 25:
How do I add room to the bust area?

If you chose a pattern according to your upper chest (see Question 20), then you may need to add room to the front bust area of your pattern. Make and try on a test garment (see Question 24); if it pulls across the bust, you need to add room in that area. If your bust measures 6.5–7.5cm (2½–3in) more than your upper chest, add 12mm (½in). If your bust measures 8–10cm (3½–4in) more than your upper chest, add 2cm (¾in). If your bust measures 11.5cm (4½in) or more than your upper chest, add 4cm (1¼in).

Lay the front pattern piece out flat – a cardboard cutting surface is ideal for this task, because you can pin the tissue in place as you work. Draw a line from the centre of the cutting line at the shoulder through the bust point to the waist, parallel to the centre-front. Draw another

line from the side seam, through the bust point to the first drawn line, bisecting any darts. Cut along these lines. Spread the pattern piece by the amount needed, keeping the vertical lines below the bust point parallel to each other. Pin down and tape tissue underneath. If your pattern has a side bust dart, it will become wider: a vertical dart, however, will be drawn back to the original size. Use the longer edge at the hem. Redraw the cutting line at the shoulder, if necessary, by adding tissue paper.

EXPERT TIP

66 Press the wrinkles out of the pattern pieces with a cool, dry iron before you begin. It helps make the alteration easier and more accurate. 99

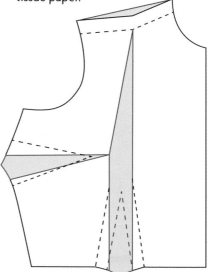

ABOVE The red shading indicates where tissue has been added to this pattern.

Question 26:
How do I make sure the bust dart is in the right place?

The point of a bust dart should end approximately 2.5cm (1in) from the tip or fullest part of your bust. To verify, compare your shoulder-to-bust-point measurement to the pattern's shoulder-to-bust-point measurement (see Question 19). If they differ, draw an X on the pattern piece where the new point should be. Then draw a box around the dart on the pattern piece (accuracy is important here) and cut out the box. Move the box up or down until the point of the dart matches the X you've drawn on the pattern, keeping the horizontal cut edges aligned. Tape in place and fill in the gaps with tissue.

If your bust points still look slightly different (which is common) when you try on the toile or garment, mark the correct point with a safety pin. Unstitch the dart and refold it to match the new point, but keep the wide part of the dart in the same place.

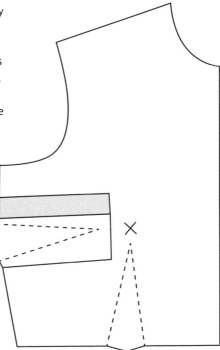

RIGHT Mark your true bust point on the front bodice piece with a cross.

Question 27:
Can I eliminate the dart?

You may have selected a type of fabric for your garment with a bold or distinctive design on it that would look wrong if folded into darts. Or you may have chosen a fabric that won't hold the dart well; it's either too stiff and unyielding, or too soft and loose. In these instances it is possible to take out a dart, but it will depend on the location.

You can try substituting gathers for a side bust dart; you will still have the fullness required, but without the line of a dart showing. When you've cut out your fabric, transfer the dart lines from the pattern to the fabric piece. When you come to sew the garment together, however, don't stitch the dart in place first. Instead, stitch a row of tacking between the dart markings at the side seam,

leaving the thread loose at both the start and finish of stitching – go beyond the markings just a bit to be sure you can gather up the thread enough. Then, when you pin the front and back sections together, pull gently on the loose threads to gather up the tacking by the same amount as the dart. When you put on the garment, the gathers will disappear into the seam. This works best with knits or soft, woven fabrics.

Another dart you can eliminate is a vertical dart on both front or back sections. There's no need to adjust the pattern tissue, just leave the dart unstitched. The waist will be less fitted, but you could take in the side seams slightly to reduce the width of the garment.

Question 28:
How do I alter my pattern for square shoulders?

Chances are, you already know if this is a fit problem for you. If your shoulders are square, draglines will appear in your garments from the wide part of your shoulder into the chest area. When making your own clothes, you can adjust the pattern to eliminate this problem.

To alter your pattern, place some tracing or tissue paper under the front bodice pattern piece at the shoulder and tape down. Draw in a new shoulder seam at a straighter angle from the neck outward (see illustration). Cut out the new section of pattern. Place some more tracing or tissue paper at the underarm and tape down. Draw in a new underarm seam that is higher by the same amount as the shoulder, so you keep the size of the armhole intact. Follow the curve or the original armhole. Cut out the new section of pattern.

Do the same thing with the back bodice pattern, altering the shoulder and underarms by the same amount as on the front piece.

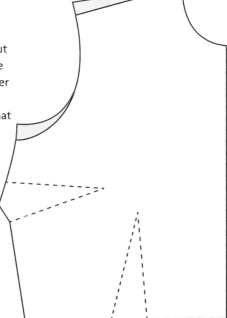

RIGHT When you raise the shoulder on a pattern you should raise the underarm by the same amount, on both front and back pieces.

Question 29:
How do I alter the pattern for sloped shoulders?

If you have particularly sloping shoulders, you may have a different problem with the fit of your clothes: draglines may appear from the neck area down toward the underarm. It may be possible to adjust this very simply with the addition of shoulder pads in a garment. You can also alter a garment pattern to correct this problem, by adjusting the shoulder seams in the reverse of Question 28.

Lay your front bodice pattern piece out flat and draw in a new shoulder seam from neck to shoulder but at a lower angle. Then redraw the armhole in a lower position; lower it by the same amount as the shoulder to keep the shape of the armhole intact. When you are happy with the alteration, trim the pattern piece to the newly drawn lines.

RIGHT When you lower the shoulder seam on both front and back pieces, lower the position of the underarm by the same amount.

Question 30:
One shoulder is higher than the other; how do I adjust the pattern?

If the difference between your two shoulders is only slight, you can try two simple shortcuts. First, insert a shoulder pad in the shoulder that is lower and that may be just enough to balance your silhouette. Alternatively, cut a bigger seam allowance at the shoulder seams when cutting out your test garment and pin the seams together on the outside before you try on the toile.

When you try on the toile, you can make the necessary changes.

Adjust the pins (in front of a mirror) on one shoulder seam, until the drag lines disappear and your silhouette is balanced. Transfer the new shoulder seam lines, front and back, to the tissue pattern pieces. Don't forget to add the same amount to the shoulder seams of the facing, if applicable. When you come to cut out the fabric (especially if cutting out a front or back in one piece) remember to cut the fabric to the adjusted pattern only on the shoulder that needs it.

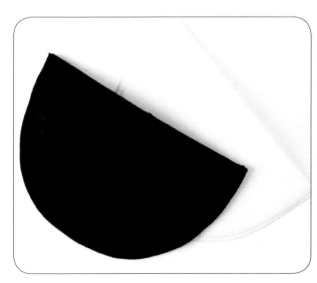

LEFT Shoulder pads are available in black or white. If you think they will show through on the right side of your garment, you could cover them with matching fabric beforehand.

Question 31:
What if my shoulders are broad?

If your shoulders are wider than the test garment, it will look and feel uncomfortable across the upper bodice. In the mirror, you will see that the edge of the shoulder or the shoulder seams (on a sleeved garment) don't reach as far as your arm joint.

Measure from the edge of the shoulder or the shoulder seam to your shoulder joint, then add a seam allowance to this measurement. This is the amount that you need to add to the front and back bodice pieces.

Place tracing or tissue paper underneath the front pattern piece at the armhole area and extend the line of the shoulder seam by the amount needed. Redraw the upper armhole curve, tapering to the original curve. Cut out the new section of pattern and tape to your pattern piece. You also need to add the same amount to the armhole on the back pattern piece so the shoulder seams match when you stitch them together.

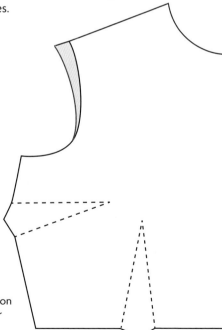

RIGHT Extending the shoulder seams on a garment will give you more room for broad shoulders.

Question 32:
What if my shoulders are narrow?

If you have narrow shoulders the top of the armhole seam on your test garment will fall beyond the end of the shoulder and will look too big. If this is a problem, mark on the test garment where your shoulder line ends at the armhole joint. Measure the distance from the fabric edge to the mark and deduct the seam allowance. This is the amount you need to take off the shoulder on both the front and back pattern pieces.

Lay the front pattern piece out flat and mark the amount you want to take off on the shoulder seam. Redraw the upper armhole, tapering down towards the underarm and following the original curve. Cut off the excess. Repeat on the back pattern piece so the shoulder seams will match when you stitch the two pieces together.

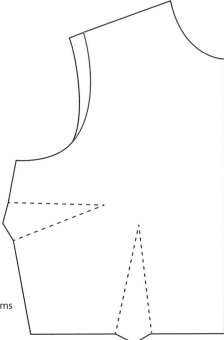

RIGHT If you adjust the shoulder seams on a garment, you will also need to redraw the armhole.

Question 33:
The back is tight; how do I add room?

If the test garment feels tight when you reach forward or if you see horizontal lines across the upper back, you need to add room to the back pattern piece. To fix this problem, first measure the width of the back pattern piece from the armhole to the centre back (do not include the seam allowance). Then take your back width measurement (see Question 19) and divide this in half. Compare the measurements; the difference between the two is what you need to add to the pattern piece.

Lay your back pattern piece out flat and draw a line from the centre point of the shoulder seam to the hem, keeping the line parallel to the lengthwise grain line. Cut the pattern in two along this line. Spread the pattern apart by the amount you need to add, making sure you keep the cut edges parallel, and then tape tracing or tissue paper in place to fill the

gap. The back shoulder seam is now wider than the front shoulder seam, so you should make a dart at the shoulder seam on the back or redraw and increase an existing dart. If you haven't added a lot, you may be able to simply ease in the excess fabric when you stitch front and back together.

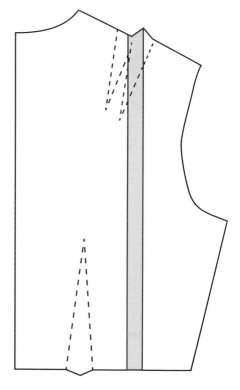

RIGHT Adding a vertical section in the back pattern piece will add ease to the back of a garment.

Question 34:
Can I change the shape of the neckline?

This is a simple design change that can be done either to the test garment or on your pattern before you cut. To change the front neckline, mark the location of the new neckline at the centre front with a dot or small line (you could hold the pattern against a favourite shop-bought top to determine this).

To lower a V-neck, redraw the neckline from the shoulder seam to the centre front mark with a straight edge. Be sure to add width for a seam allowance. To raise a V-neck, add tissue underneath the pattern and then draw in a new neckline.

Cut off excess tissue along the new neckline. You can use the same technique to raise or lower a round neckline but use a curved ruler to draw the curve from the shoulder to centre front.

You can do the same in the test garment; fold it in half exactly along the centre front and tack on some extra fabric to the chest area. Draw the new neckline from shoulder to centre front. Don't forget to add a seam allowance.

EXPERT TIP

❝ If you need a neck facing, use the adjusted front piece as a guide to create a new pattern piece. Pin the new front piece (still folded at the centre front) on tissue paper. Trace the new neck edge from the shoulder to the centre front. Draw a new line 7.5cm (3in) in from the neck edge to make the outer edge of the pattern. Cut out the tissue to make the facing pattern. ❞

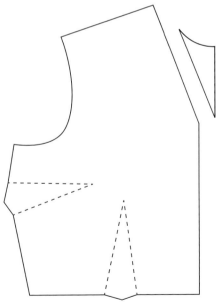

ABOVE The neckline of a front pattern piece is easily refashioned.

Question 35:
Where is my natural waist?

It is important to know where your true, natural waist lies so that you can make an accurate comparison of your measurement to the pattern measurement. Current fashion trends have blurred the definition of a true waistline with terms like low-rise, mid-rise or high-rise. Your true waist is not necessarily where you wear your favourite jeans!

To locate your natural waist, tie a length of elastic around your waist. The elastic will settle comfortably at the narrowest part of your torso; this is your true waist. You can also stand up in front of a mirror and bend sideways; the 'crease' in your torso where you bend is your true waist. Whichever method you use, your natural waist is where you should place the tape measure for accuracy. You should also compare the position of your natural waist in relation to your neck or to the ground with the position of the waistline markings on your pattern.

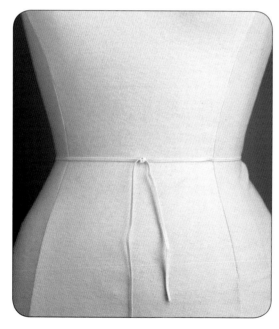

LEFT Tie a length of elastic around your waist to determine your true waistline. Fasten it so that clings very slightly to your body, and isn't too tight or too loose.

Question 36:
The waist on my pattern is too high; how do I fix this?

You are considered long-waisted if the waist of shirts, tops or dresses falls above your natural waist. Garments that are too short in your torso are uncomfortable and unflattering. Compare the back-neck to waist measurement on your chart (see Question 19) to the same measurement listed on the pattern size chart. Sometimes this measurement is shown on the back of the pattern envelope under 'Finished Garment Measurements', below the yardage chart. The difference between the two measurements is the amount you need to lower the waist.

Lay the front pattern piece out flat and draw a horizontal line across the middle of the pattern just above the waistline. Make sure the line is perpendicular to the lengthwise grain line (look for lengthening/shortening lines which may already be marked on the pattern pieces). Cut the pattern piece in two along this line. Spread the upper and lower pieces apart

by the amount needed. Tape tissue paper underneath, making sure the two edges you cut remain exactly parallel. You may need to redraw the cutting line at the side. Repeat with the back pattern piece, making sure you draw your horizontal line in the same position as on the front: all bodice pieces must be changed by the same amount.

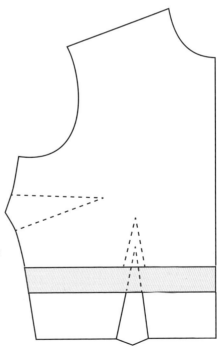

RIGHT After lengthening your pattern, redraw the darts to the same size.

Question 37:

The waist on my pattern is too low; how do I raise it?

If you are petite or 'short-waisted' then the waistline on garments will probably fall below your natural waist. Compare your back-neck to waist measurements to those given on the pattern, as in Question 36. The difference between the two measurements is the amount you need to raise the waist.

Lay the front pattern piece out flat and draw two parallel lines just above the waistline, perpendicular to the lengthwise grain line. The distance between the two lines should be the amount you need to raise your waist. (The pattern may already have a lengthen/shorten line printed on each pattern piece.

If so, draw a second line above it.) Fold the tissue along the lower line and bring the fold up to the other line; tape the fold in place. You may need to straighten the pattern at the side seam. Repeat with the back pattern piece, making sure you draw your lines in the same position as the front piece and that the size of the fold is the same.

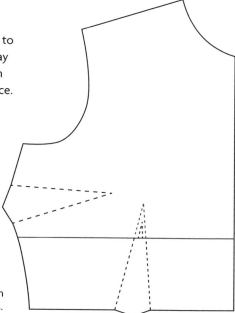

RIGHT After folding up your pattern piece to shorten it, redraw any darts.

Question 38:
Can I make the waist bigger or smaller?

A simple way to add room at the waist is to leave darts unstitched. You could also make darts smaller, and therefore take in less fabric.

If your hipline and waist tend to be straight rather than curved, you can add room at the side seam. Work out how much you want to increase the waistline and divide this by four, since you will be adding to both side seams on both pattern pieces. If, for example, you want to add 5cm (2in), you will need to add 12mm (½in) to the side seam at front and back. Lay the front piece out flat and tape tissue underneath

the side seam. Redraw the side seam starting at the widest part of the hipline and widen towards the waistline to the measurement required. Repeat this on the back pattern piece.

You can reduce the waist in a similar way. Work out how much you want to take off and divide this by four. Then lay out the front pattern piece and make a mark on the waistline this measurement in from the side seam. Redraw the side seam from this mark, tapering down towards the hip. Trim off the excess. Repeat with the back pattern piece.

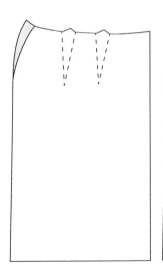
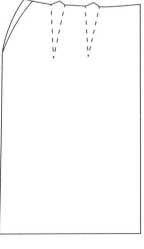

LEFT Add tissue at the waist and hip (see far left) to add more room at the waistline. Reduce the waistline and redraw the side seam (see near left) to make the waist smaller.

Question 39:
How do I adjust the fit at the hip?

You may need to add room in the hip area only and still keep the fit intact at the waistline. To determine how much room you need, compare your hip measurement to the pattern size chart. If you have a multi-size pattern, the change is easy to do. When you cut the pattern tissue pieces, follow the lines that match the size you need in the waist, and then flare out to the size you need at the hip. For example, if your waist is a size 10 according to the chart and your hips are a size 12, cut along the size 10 at the waist, and widen out to the size 12 line at the hip and for the rest of the pattern.

If your pattern does not have multi-size lines, you will need to add tissue to the front and back pattern pieces at the side seam.

Divide the total amount you need to add by four and then add that amount of tissue to the side seams at the hip line. Draw the new seam line so it lies parallel to the existing seam line as it runs down to the hem and so that it tapers to nothing as it meets the waist.

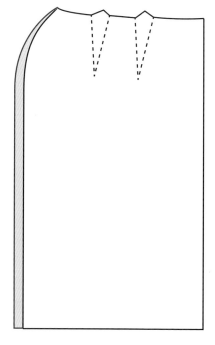

RIGHT If you are wide around the hips, you can increase the size of the pattern at this point, but keep to the original measurements at the waist.

Question 40:
How do I adjust the length of skirts, dresses and trousers?

Most commercial patterns are printed with horizontal lines labelled 'lengthen or shorten here', which takes away the guesswork of knowing where to adjust the length of a garment. It may seem easier at times to just add or cut off some of the length at the bottom edge of a pattern piece but this may distort the intended design of the garment. For example, a flared skirt will lose its fullness if you shorten the pattern pieces by cutting off the bottom.

When you extend or shorten the length of a pattern piece the vertical edges, such as the side seams, may become distorted and should be redrawn to create a smooth transition top to bottom. This is called 'truing' the seam.

EXPERT TIP

66 Length adjustments usually have to be made to more than one pattern piece, so if you are tall, purchase extra fabric. 99

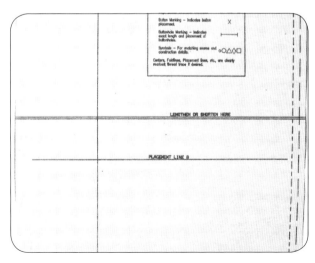

LEFT The place where you can lengthen or shorten a pattern is often clearly marked.

Question 41:
How do I change the sleeve length?

A long-sleeve pattern piece will usually be marked with a 'lengthen/shorten here' line to help you make an adjustment. To determine any changes you need to make to a long-sleeve first take your arm measurement: measure from the top of the arm to the elbow and from the elbow to the wrist; combine the two for your total arm length. Then measure the length of the sleeve pattern piece and compare the two to work out how much needs to be added or subtracted. On a fitted long sleeve, there may be two 'lengthen/shorten here' lines, one above and one below the elbow. If this is the case, then you should make adjustments at both of these lines.

To add length, slash through the horizontal line (or lines) and spread the pattern by the amount needed. Keep the lines parallel to each other and tape tissue in the space.

To shorten the sleeve, draw a second horizontal line on the pattern at a distance equal to the change you need to make. Fold on one line and bring the fold up to meet the other

horizontal line. Press the folds with a cool, dry iron and tape in place. When making a change in two places, verify the change against your total arm length.

If the change you need to make is only slight, or if your pattern has short sleeves, you can add or subtract the extra amount at the hem edge. Be sure to add 2.5–4cm (1–1½in) for the hem allowance.

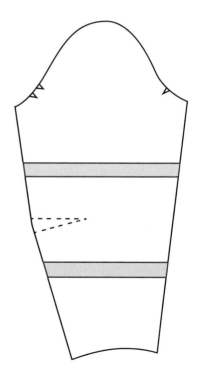

RIGHT Add tissue at the 'lengthen/shorten here' lines to increase a sleeve.

Question 42:
How do I make the sleeves bigger?

A sleeve that is too tight is difficult to get into. To make your sleeve bigger in the upper arms, first measure the width across the sleeve pattern from corner to corner where the arm curve meets the side seam. Compare that to your arm circumference, plus 5in (2in) for ease. The difference between the two measurements is the amount you need to add to the sleeve pattern.

Lay the pattern out flat and draw a line from the dot at the centre top of the sleeve cap to the centre of the wrist, parallel to the lengthwise grainline. Draw another line across the sleeve cap, roughly halfway between the notches and the centre dot, that bisects and is perpendicular to the first line.

Cut along the vertical line from the wrist, until you nearly reach the centre dot at the sleeve top: don't cut right through. Cut into the pattern at the horizontal line (which has now been bisected) until you nearly reach the edge of the pattern; again, don't cut right through. You will have a cross-shaped cut. Put tissue paper under

the slash and then spread it open at the top, keeping the cut edges at the wrist together. (You could use some sticky tape to keep the cut together at the wrist.) You should end up with an extended diamond shape as the pieces open up. The amount you need to add should be the same as the diamond's widest point. The top of the sleeve cap will have been lowered so you need to redraw this to its original shape.

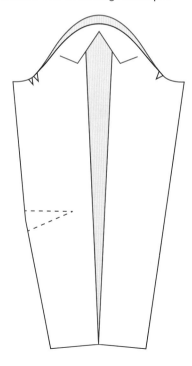

RIGHT You need to add room at the top of a sleeve for full upper arms.

Question 43:
The armholes are tight; what should I do?

You will discover if this is a problem after you have sewn the side seams together in the test garment. The lower curve of the armhole (between the front and back notches and the sleeve side seams) needs to be reshaped so the finished sleeve does not cut into your armpit.

Lay the front and back bodice pieces on a flat surface and redraw the lower curve from each notch to the side seam. Be sure to include seam allowances after you draw the new stitch line or the finished curve will be too low. Trim the pattern along the new line.

If your style has a set-in sleeve, you will also have to change the curve of the sleeve to match the bigger armhole. Redraw the lower curve of the sleeve from the notch to the sleeve seam on either side by the same amount you lowered the armhole. Trim the pattern to the new line. For a sleeveless style that has an armhole facing, redraw the facing curve by the same amount.

RIGHT You should adjust the sleeve by the same amount as the bodice.

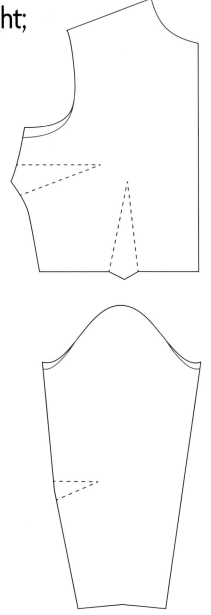

Question 44:
My bra shows at the underarms; how do I eliminate this?

You may have the opposite problem from that in Question 43 if you are shorter between your shoulders and underarms than the pattern. The adjustment is different and is done on the pattern pieces for the sleeve, and the front and the back bodice.

First, measure with a ruler how much you wish to raise the armhole to cover your undergarment. This may not be apparent until you are wearing the test garment.

To alter the pattern, lay all three pattern pieces – front, back, and sleeve – on your flat surface and draw a horizontal line through each one halfway between the shoulder seam and the notches. This line should be perpendicular to the lengthwise grainline. Slash through each line and then overlap each pattern by the amount you wish to reduce the pattern. Tape the pattern pieces in place, then redraw the side seams and the curves of the armhole and sleeve top so they are neat and even. Trim the pattern pieces to the new lines.

RIGHT Shorten bodice pieces and sleeves to raise the underarm.

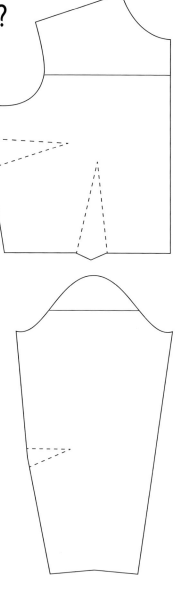

PREPARING AND CUTTING FABRIC

Question 45:
How do I match the right fabric to my pattern?

Choosing fabric is one of the most enjoyable aspects of dressmaking, although you may be overwhelmed by the colours, patterns and textures available in fabric stores. Pattern companies try to help you with this task by suggesting suitable fabrics on the back of the pattern envelope; you'll find this information in a box above the fabric quantity chart.

The best way to find the right fabric is to spend time looking at – and touching – materials. It's not a good idea to deviate too much from the suggested fabric, but you'll want to choose one that you like. Information on the pattern will also tell you what to avoid, such

EXPERT TIP

❝ Patterns are designed either for knit or woven fabric and should not be confused. If the pattern is designed for a knit it will specifically recommend knits in the fabric box. It will also include a stretch factor gauge on the back of the pattern envelope for you to test the fabric's stretch. Choosing the wrong fabric in this case will compromise the fit of your garment. ❞

as obvious diagonals or plaids for certain styles. (See Question 23 for suggestions on how to choose flattering patterns and fabrics.)

LEFT Many fabric types come in a wide range of colours, so there's something available to suit everyone.

Question 46:
What fabrics should I avoid if this is my first project?

Some fabrics are indeed trickier to sew than others. To ensure success, choose a fabric that is medium weight, with a design that is not too large – the motifs can look very different on a body than on a bolt of cloth. Avoid fabrics that are shiny or slippery – such as silk, chiffon, or satin – or too thin. Working with plaids or other obvious horizontal prints can also be tricky, so you may want to save these for the future.

Choose a fabric on which it is easy to tell the right (outer) side from the wrong (inner) side. If a fabric looks similar on both sides it is easy to confuse the two when you are assembling pieces, and when you have to sew 'right sides together' you could get it wrong.

Question 47:
Is there anything I should do to the fabric before I begin?

Before you cut your fabric, wash and dry it in the same way that you plan to wash the finished garment. If there is going to be any shrinkage, you want this to happen before you make up the garment, not after!

Fabrics that are dry cleanable such as wool and certain types of silk, can be 'pre-shrunk' by hand at the ironing board. Fill the iron with water for steam and lay the fabric out on the ironing board.

Hold the iron about 2 inches above the fabric surface and apply steam throughout. Before moving the fabric, let it dry. Some silk fabric can be hand washed and air-dried.

Most fabrics, even cottons, do not shrink much, but some materials have a finish on the surface, and after washing this may soften up. If the fabric is wrinkled after washing and drying, press it before you begin the layout process.

Question 48:
What do the terms 'selvage' and 'grain line' mean?

Selvage refers to the manufactured edge of your fabric as it comes off the bolt. If your fabric has been previously cut, you may no longer have a selvage, but it is an important term to remember. The selvage always runs parallel to the lengthwise grain of the fabric – the direction of the warp threads in woven fabrics. The crosswise grain, formed by the weft threads, is perpendicular to the selvage.

A third type of grain line is the bias grain, which intersect the lengthwise and crosswise grains at a 45-degree angle. These three grain lines exist in all woven fabrics, and cutting out your pattern on the correct grain lines will ensure that the final garment looks, feels, and drapes the way the designer (and you) intended.

EXPERT TIP

66 **Generally speaking, the selvage is easy to find on printed woven fabrics – the manufacturer's name and a colour code is printed on that edge. 99**

LEFT In a fabric where the warp and weft threads are two different colours, here black and pink, it is easy to see the selvage. The black, warp threads form the lengthwise grain; the pink, weft threads form the crosswise grain.

Question 49:
What is the bias?

All woven fabrics (not knits) have lengthwise and crosswise grain lines, following the lengthwise and crosswise threads that create the weave of the fabric. If you pull the fabric in either of these directions, you will find that has very little stretch or give. (The exception to this is fabric that contains Lycra, which is added to many woven fabrics today to create some stretch.)

The bias is the third type of grain line on a woven fabric and it lies between the lengthwise and crosswise grains at a 45-degree angle. To find the true bias grain, bring the selvage of the fabric (see Question 48) and place it along the crosswise grain or weave. The diagonal fold you create is following the true bias grain line. If you take either end of the fold and pull gently, it stretches, unlike the other two grain lines. A dress or skirt cut along the bias grain drapes and hangs more softly than garments cut on the lengthwise grain, and because of the extra give, less fitting elements are required, such as darts, seams, or pleats. The best patterns to use on the bias grain are those with simple lines and few details.

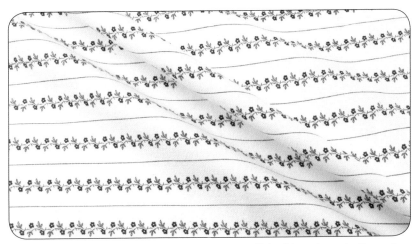

ABOVE To check that you've found the bias grain, pull the fabric along the line and you will see that it stretches easily.

Question 50:
How do I lay out my pattern pieces?

Now that you have your pattern adjusted, and your fabric washed and ready, it's time to layout and pin your pattern to the fabric. Commercial patterns contain a guide sheet with a diagram of how to lay each pattern piece on your fabric. Take note of the words 'fold' and 'selvage' in each diagram. Fold your fabric so that the selvages meet (see Question 48) and the fold is opposite and parallel to the selvage.

On the pattern information sheet, there will be several diagrams to choose from, depending on the width of your chosen fabric, and on the size and garment view you are making. Find the diagram that corresponds with each of these elements and circle it with pen so you don't lose your place when you refer to it during the layout process. Follow the diagram as you place your pattern pieces on the fabric. Pattern pieces are numbered and are listed with the correct diagram, so be sure you have the ones you need. Each pattern piece also tells you how many of each piece to cut. For example, 'Cut 2' will appear on a sleeve pattern piece. If you have folded your fabric, you will lay the pattern out once and cut through two layers to get two pieces.

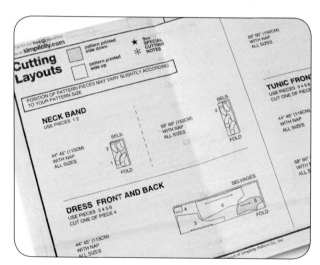

LEFT On the guide sheet inside your pattern envelope you will find diagrams that show how to lay out the pattern pieces on the fabric.

Question 51:
How do I cut accurately on the grain line?

Proper placement of pattern pieces on the grain line of the fabric is one of the most important steps in the cutting stage of your project. If the grain lines are not followed, your garment will not hang properly and any vertical designs on the fabric will look askew. Every pattern piece is printed with a line, with directional arrows at each end, to help you position the piece correctly on the grain. The pattern piece must be placed on the fabric so that the grain line on the tissue is parallel to the selvage of the fabric.

HERE'S HOW

First pin the pattern to the fabric at one end of the grain line. Measure from this end of the grain line (see right) to the edge of the fabric – it can be either the selvage or the folded edge. Move your tape measure or ruler to the other end of the grain line and measure to the same fabric edge. You want the two measurements to be the same so move the unpinned end of the grain line until is is the same distance from the fabric edge as the pinned end. Pin this end of the grain line through all layers and then pin the whole pattern piece in place.

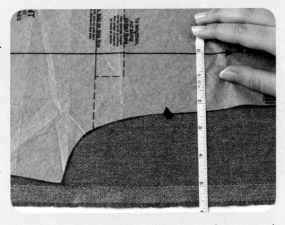

Question 52:
What does 'cut on fold' mean?

These words are printed on some pattern pieces along with a line that has directional arrows at each end; the arrows tell you which direction the piece should face the fabric fold. You need to pin the relevant edge of the pattern piece exactly along the fold of the fabric.

When all pattern pieces are pinned, cut the 'on fold' pieces around the remaining edges but not along the fold line. When you open out the fabric piece, you will see that it is one piece, not two. Some pattern pieces will instruct you to 'cut two on fold'. This means you cut the pattern out twice, each time placing it along the fold. Look for this on smaller pattern pieces, such as collars and cuffs.

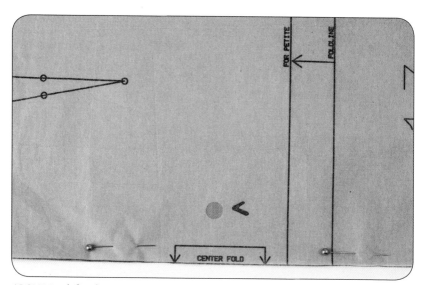

ABOVE Look for the instruction 'cut on fold' or 'centre fold' and pin this edge of the pattern along the fold of your fabric.

Question 53:
What is the best way to pin down the pattern pieces?

Once you have your pattern pieces properly laid out on the fabric (see Question 50), you need pin the paper to the fabric, pinning through all the layers. The first two pins should be on the grain lines (see Question 48). Then pin around the pattern, close to the cutting edge but not so the pins extend beyond the edge of the tissue; space the pins 5–7.5cm (2–3in) apart. Many beginners do not use enough pins to secure the pattern to the fabric, which can cause the pattern to move when cutting out and result in inaccurately cut garment pieces.

Always lay the fabric and pattern on a firm, flat surface and pierce through all layers twice when you pin – once downwards, towards the table, and once back up through the fabric, away from the table. Smooth out the layers with the palms of your hands as you pin. Do not over pin as this distorts and wrinkles the fabric. Put your other hand under the fabric as little as possible, as this also distorts the fabric and pattern.

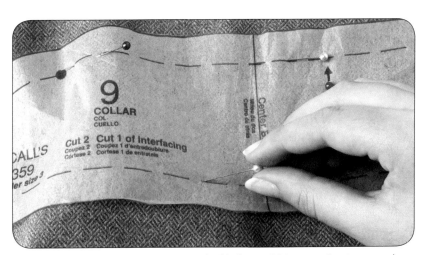

ABOVE If you are pinning a pattern to a double layer of fabric, as when instructed to 'Cut 2', make sure you pin through all layers.

Question 54:
My pattern envelope contains several pieces; do I use all of them?

Sewing patterns usually come with several garment style choices in one envelope and so you will only need the pattern pieces for your chosen style: you will not need every pattern piece! The guide sheet in your pattern envelope will indicate exactly what ones you need. All the pieces are numbered and will be listed in the layout diagram for your chosen style, your size, and the width of your fabric.

In some patterns, you will get separate pieces for each size that is provided, so take care to verify the correct size when cutting out those pieces. These are usually the collar and collar band; you may also find some patterns that contain a different front bodice piece for each bra-cup size. Make sure you cut out the right piece for your particular cup size.

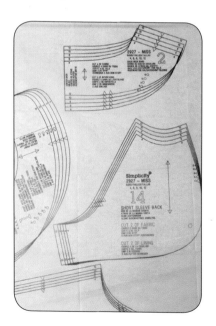

EXPERT TIP

66 When you've cut out the pieces you need to make your chosen garment, store them separately from the unused pieces in case you need to refer back to them quickly later on. 99

LEFT Inside your pattern envelope you will find large sheets of tissue, printed with every pattern piece needed for every view offered by that pattern. You need only cut out the pieces for your chosen garment.

Question 55:
There are various markings on my pattern pieces; what do they mean?

Pattern pieces are printed with a variety of symbols that serve as a guide to stitching your garment together in the proper order. Your pattern guide sheet will refer to these markings and tell you how to use them as you assemble the garment pieces.

Transferring all these marks to your fabric before starting to sew can seem tedious and it may be tempting to skip this stage. However, it saves time in the long run as you'll only have to return to the pattern pieces to verify how the fabric pieces are put together.

Around the edges of pattern pieces you will see triangle or diamond shapes; these are known as notches. They are used to match one pattern piece to another: for example, the notches at the top of a sleeve should be matched to the notches at the armhole edge of the bodice. They appear singly, in pairs, or in threes; single notches should be matched to single notches, double notches to double notches, triples to triples.

Darts are indicated with solid or dotted lines and usually feature a dot or small circle at the point, and along the lines. You'll also find other dots or circles that help you to mark the position of other essential features, including waistbands, pockets and closures.

Question 56:
How do I mark darts?

The best way to mark darts is with carbon tracing paper and a wheel (see Question 13) because it is the most accurate technique. However, you can still mark darts successfully with a few pins and tailor's chalk or a marking pencil.

The most common type of darts are side bust darts, waist darts, elbow darts and shoulder darts. On a pattern, they look like a narrow pie shape formed by two dotted lines that start at a seam and meet at a point. A contoured dart runs vertically from the bust to the hips with a wider centre at the waist; this type of dart is roughly diamond in shape. Because it is longer than most darts, you may need to use two pieces of tracing paper to place between the layers of fabric before you mark with a wheel.

Darts also have large dots spaced along the stitch lines for

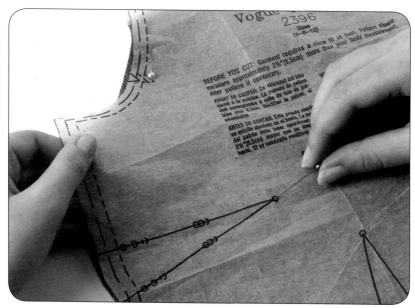

ABOVE To mark a dot, stick a pin in the dot and lift up the pattern piece and then the top layer of fabric. Rub chalk on both pieces of fabric where pierced by the pin.

EXPERT TIP

66 A time saver for marking darts is to place a small snip in the seam allowance where the dart lines begin. Be careful not to snip more than 3mm (⅛in). Mark the points with pins and chalk as described above. 99

easy marking with just pins and tailor's chalk. Stick a pin in each dot, through all layers (tissue and fabric). Peel back one layer of fabric and use tailor's chalk to mark where each pin intersects the fabric pieces. The dots form the dart shape when you connect them. You can stitch as is, or draw in the lines with tailor's chalk for a more precise stitching guide.

Question 57:
How do I mark pleats?

Pleats are a wonderful design feature that can add fullness to a garment at the waist, shoulders and wrists. For the best results, use carbon tracing paper and wheel for accurate marking or snip the seam allowance, as described in the Tip with Question 56.

Pleats may or may not be stitched on the vertical lines shown on the pattern – they may be just folded on the lines indicated and then stitched across the folds to hold in place. Either way, pleats must be folded as accurately as marked before being stitched. Also, pay attention to how they are to be folded; the pattern will indicate with arrows the direction in which they should be folded and pressed.

EXPERT TIP

66 Pairs or sets of design details that are placed on both sides of a garment must be sewn so they form mirror images of each other – they should face in opposite directions to one another. For example, if the wrist pleats on one sleeve are pressed to the left, they should be pressed to the right on the opposite sleeve. 99

Question 58:
What are notches for and how do I mark them?

Notches are single, double, or triple diamond or triangle shapes around the perimeter of the pattern pieces. These marks help you to pin and sew the right pattern pieces to one another. They are like puzzle pieces that help you fit the garment together properly.

Notches are often drawn inward on the pattern piece, but they should be cut outward in fabric to preserve the width of seam allowances. They can be cut across the top, as long as you do make them as wide as indicated. You should be able to distinguish the width of them, since singles are matched to singles, and doubles are matched to doubles, and so on. They are a must to help keep you from mixing up sleeves, or cuffs or other 'pairs' of pattern pieces.

EXPERT TIP

66 If you forget to cut them, you can simply mark the location of the notches with tailor's chalk before you unpin pattern pieces from fabric. 99

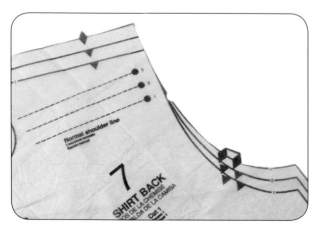

LEFT The single notches on this pattern will help match front and back pieces. The double notches will help with fitting the sleeve into the armhole.

Question 59:
How do I keep the fabric from slipping?

Some fabrics such as chiffon, silk charmeuse, organza or other lightweight materials and sheers have more movement than others and may slide around during the cutting process. To minimise this, pin the two layers of fabric together along the selvage, smoothing it flat with your hands. If you are on a cardboard surface, pin the fabric layers down around the edges. You can also machine tack around the perimeter of the fabric to hold the layers together.

When cutting out, a rotary cutter is a good option because the fabric remains flat as you cut. If you use dressmaking shears, keep the blades flat against the cutting surface and cut with long, even strokes. The idea is to keep the fabric from lifting as little as possible.

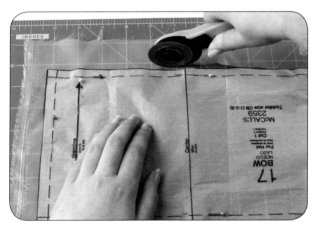

LEFT If using a rotary cutter, place the fabric on a self-healing mat or cardboard cutting mat to protect your work surface.

EXPERT TIP

❝ Try placing tissue paper underneath the fabric before you begin and cut through all layers of fabric, pattern and tissue. You can successfully cut out tricky fabrics with patience and good cutting tools. ❞

Question 60:
How do I cut out stretchy, knit fabrics?

Stretchy fabrics such as slinky knits or sweater knits need to be handled differently than more stable knits such as sweatshirt fabric and cotton jersey. When you lay the fabric out, make sure it does not hang down over the edge of your table, as the weight causes distortion of the material. As with slippery woven fabrics (see Question 59), a rotary cutter provides a clean cut and keeps the fabric flat on the cutting surface as you work.

EXPERT TIP

66 **With some knits it's difficult to distinguish the right from the wrong side. If you stretch a knit along the fabric edge it curls toward the right side.** 99

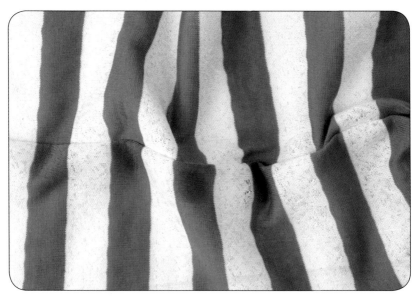

ABOVE Knit fabrics are soft and drape well, creating a flattering fit. They can, however, be difficult to cut out since they move easily on the cutting surface.

Question 61:
What if the print on the fabric points in one direction only?

If your fabric has a print that is directional or one-way — for example, featuring tree-tops pointing in the same direction — place your pattern pieces on the fabric so that the top of each piece points in the same direction as the top of each design/motif. If you fail to do this, the design might be upside down when you wear the garment, or it might run in a different direction on the front and another direction on the back!

This is not a concern with 'all-over' fabric designs, but if you do select a fabric with a 'one-way' design, purchase an extra 25–50cm (10–20in) of fabric to allow for any extra you may need to lay out the pattern pieces in one direction only. Check the back of the pattern envelope for fabric amounts under the heading 'with nap'. Since the nap on a fabric (see Question 64) runs in one direction only, the fabric amounts needed will be the same.

LEFT Some fabrics feature designs, such as this floral pattern, that have a distinct top and bottom, and which need to be cut out with care.

Question 62:
What if the fabric incorporates a border design?

Some fabrics include a border design, which runs along the selvage. The pattern is usually cut so that the border design runs along the hem of the finished garment. The pattern pieces, therefore, must be cut on the crosswise grain. Since the crosswise grain has a little more stretch or give than the lengthwise grain (though not as much as the bias grain), the fit of the garment may be slightly different. It should not, however, require you to make any changes to the pattern.

LEFT Some fabrics feature a striking border design that looks perfect when placed at the hem edge of a skirt or dress, or when running around the bottom of a shirt.

EXPERT TIP

66 To keep the flow of the design consistent across the garment, you may want to ensure that any pattern that has a zip closure has this in the side seam instead of the back seam. It's also wise to check the finished hem edge along the border print, so you don't lose some of the design in the hem allowance. 99

Question 63:
How do I cut out check or tartan fabrics?

Working with plaids and tartans requires extra care when positioning your pattern pieces on the fabric. You will need to purchase extra fabric for matching plaids – 25–50cm (10–20in) more, depending on how large the design is. Follow the pattern guide sheet for the layout of pieces on one-way designs.

First, fold the fabric so that the plaid lines match up horizontally on both layers: look to the selvages to verify. At the same time, the fold should be centred vertically down the middle of a plaid design. This will ensure that when a pattern piece is cut on the fold – such as the centre front or back – the design will be centred on the body.

When placing pattern pieces on the fabric, align them on the same horizontal line so that when the fabric pieces are sewn together, they match up. For example, the front and back pieces of a dress pattern should be placed on the same horizontal line at the corners of the side seams.

EXPERT TIP

❝ **When you first work with a plaid fabric, choose one with a small design, and go for a garment pattern that has just a few main pieces.** ❞

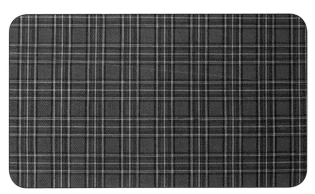

LEFT With plaids and tartans the design is usually woven into the fabric, rather than printed, making it easier to fold fabric accurately along the checks.

Question 64:
What is 'nap' and how do I cut out fabric with a nap?

Napped fabrics have a texture that feels 'rough' when you run your hand in one direction along the lengthwise grain, and 'smooth' when you run your hand in the opposite lengthwise direction. The fabric will also look a slightly different colour in opposing directions. When you cut out your pattern pieces, therefore, the nap should run in the same direction on each part of the garment, or the finished item will look as if it's made up of different pieces of fabric. Velvet, velveteen, corduroy, some types of fleece and faux fur all have distinct naps.

Since the nap on this kind of fabric runs in one direction, the pattern pieces should be laid out on the fabric so the top of each piece points in the same direction. You'll need to buy slightly more fabric with a nap to compensate for the restrictions on laying out the pattern, but you should find a guide to how much is needed on the pattern envelope. (See also Question 61.)

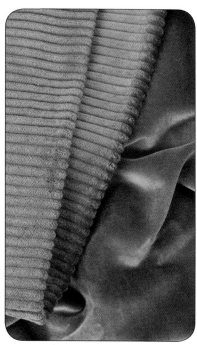

ABOVE Both corduroy and velvet have a raised pile that is known as the nap.

Question 65:
I don't have enough fabric! What should I do?

At some point, you will likely experience the scenario where you have a wonderful fabric in hand, ready to cut and sew, but the pattern calls for more fabric than you have. If this happens you may well think of abandoning the project. But don't despair until you have considered the following options.

You could try making the smaller pieces of the garment – such as the cuffs, collars, pockets, or yokes – out of a different fabric. This could be one that matches the main fabric or is a complete contrast. A white collar and cuffs, for example, can look striking on a patterned blouse.

Another option would be to split part of the pattern (adding a seam allowance) in a hidden place and cut one of the pieces in a different fabric. For example, you could cut a wedge at the corner of a wide skirt where the side seam and hem meet.

If you are only just short of material, you could save fabric at the seams of a garment by joining pieces together with a trim or a band of contrasting fabric. You could also use a different material for facings or for the underside of those parts of a garment that are made in two parts, such as collars, cuffs and waistbands. Just remember to choose a fabric that's a similar weight and composition to the main fabric. If you're making a shirt out of a fine cotton, for example, it would be inappropriate to use a woollen fabric as a facing or to back collars and cuffs.

Why not consider a design change? Shorten the sleeves or the length of a skirt; make a top instead of a dress. Whatever you decide, see this an opportunity to be creative and the result could be more exciting than you thought.

MACHINE STITCHING

4

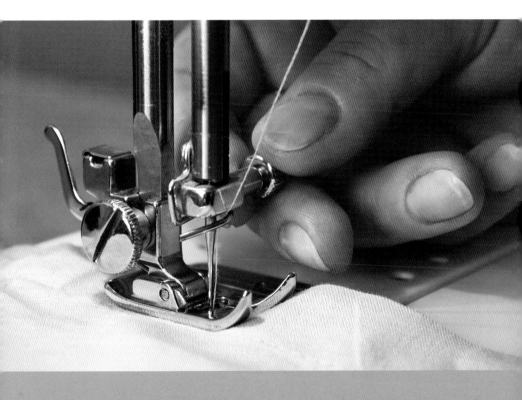

Question 66:
I am ready to begin sewing; what do I do first?

Before you begin your project, check your sewing machine settings. Have you got the right type of stitch selected and is the stitch length set properly? Do a test stitch on a scrap of fabric — it should be the same fabric that you are using for your garment — to check that the thread tension is correct. Is it time to change the needle? If it's necessary, insert a new one before you begin.

Many beginners are nervous about unpinning and removing the pattern pieces from the cut fabric. If you are concerned about mixing up your pieces or not knowing which ones are which, you can label them with a marking pencil in the seam allowance. For example, use B for back; F for front; R for right; and L for left.

Pin the pieces of fabric right sides together before you sew. Have your iron set up ready to press the seams flat after you've sewn them together. The first step in garment construction is usually to sew together any darts, followed by stitching together the largest sections. However, the pattern guide sheet should give you complete instructions on the order in which to assemble your garment.

Question 67:
What is hand tacking, and when do I use it?

There are several types of hand sewing stitches that might be needed when constructing a garment. Hand tacking is sewing a simple running stitch with a needle and thread, usually through two or more layers of fabric. It is used to temporarily hold fabric pieces together before stitching permanently by machine. Use a long, medium-thickness needle and a contrasting thread, so the tacking can be easily seen and removed.

It may also be used on a single layer to mark a line when using a chalk or fabric marker would not be advisable. Some fabrics are difficult to mark such as a tweed or bouclé, or you may be concerned as to whether the chalk or marker will wash out completely. A length of tacking stitches can also be used to gather up fabric if, say, you need to ease the fullness of a sleeve into the armhole of a bodice, or to gather up the fabric in a full-waisted skirt.

ABOVE Hand tacking is easy to do. Secure the thread with a few small stitches and then run the needle in and out of the fabric, before pulling the thread through.

Question 68:
What stitch length should I set on my machine?

Most seams require a stitch length setting of 2.5. Your stitch length dial is typically located on the right side of your machine as a large knob, or along the top of your machine as a dial. An icon usually appears as a dotted line that stretches as the stitch length increases. Generally speaking, the stitch length ranges from 1.0 to 4.0, although sewing machines will vary.

If you need to machine tack, this generally means a setting of 4.0 on most stitch length dials. The smallest stitch is 1.0. Experience will tell you when to adjust your stitch length, but most of the time, you will sew on a 2.5 stitch setting.

Question 69:
What is a zigzag stitch and when do I use it?

The zigzag function on your machine is part of the stitch width control and is usually marked with a zigzag icon that moves from narrow to wide so you can adjust as needed. You can also change the distance between the zigzags by adjusting the stitch length at the same time. Test stitch before using on your garment so you can see the finished result.

This is a versatile stitch that can be utilised in many ways. You can stitch seams on knits with a narrow setting to give a bit of give to the seam. This stitch is also useful for

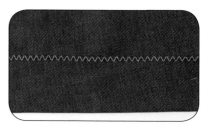

ABOVE Use zigzag stitch to both secure a hem and finish the raw edge.

finishing seam allowances on woven fabrics: select a wide stitch and then centre the edge of the seam allowance under the needle so that the needle goes in and then off the fabric with each stitch. This helps 'wrap' the raw edge with thread to reduce frayed seams.

There are several decorative stitches on my machine; when do I use these?

Decorative stitches are a great way to enhance your garments and most sewing machine models offer a variety of options. You don't need fancy thread or special needles to achieve great results.

If you're thinking of using a decorative stitch, always do a test sample on a spare scrap of your fabric before using it on your final garment. If the stitches look bunched up or distorted, add a stabiliser under your fabric: this could be a piece of lightweight interfacing or a scrap of very fine fabric, such as organza. If you stitch a design on to a part of the garment that already includes interfacing – such as a collar, cuff, or waistband – you won't need to add a stabiliser. When you do your test sample, experiment with different stitch lengths and widths too. Adding even the simplest of decorative stitches can make a garment look truly unique and feel 'custom' made.

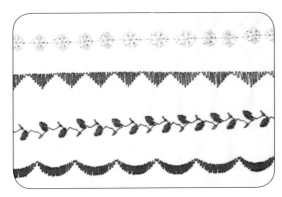

LEFT You can use decorative stitches instead of straight stitches to add interest when sewing a hem or finishing a cuff.

Question 71:
What is stay stitching?

Stay stitching is a singe line of stitching done through a single layer of fabric in order to keep curved or bias edges from stretching out of shape as you handle the garment. Its purpose is just what the name implies – to help fabric edges stay in place.

Not all pattern guide sheets include this step, but it is an important one that should not be skipped. Develop the good habit of stay stitching around the curves and angles of your garment pieces before you join them together. Examples of where to stay stitch include V-shaped necklines, round necklines, slanted pocket edges, and curved waistlines, all of which have bias edges. This simple step will save you frustration and avoid unattractive results in the long run.

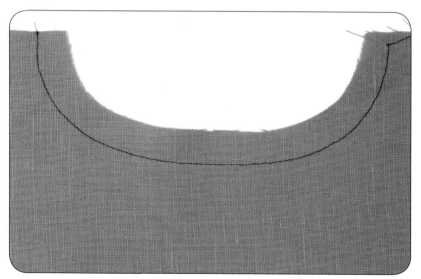

ABOVE Before stitching together any curved garment pieces, stay stitch around the curve, just within the seam allowance.

Question 72:
What is a backstitch or backtack?

Backstitching, also know as backtacking, is the process of stitching in reverse at the beginning and end of a seam to keep the stitches from coming out. Not to be confused with a hand or embroidery stitch of the same name, it is done with the sewing machine using a normal stitch length.

To backstitch, begin sewing your seam forward for three to four stitches, then press the reverse button on your sewing machine and hold it down for two to three stitches. Release and continue stitching forward to the end of the seam. At the end of your seam, press and hold the reverse button again to stitch backwards two to three stitches. Release and stitch to the end again, over the previous stitches. This is an essential part of sewing a seam that will soon become a habit, as easy as threading your needle. It is not necessary to backstitch when sewing on a single layer of fabric, as in stay stitching or tacking. Just remember to do this step whenever you are sewing two or more layers of fabric together.

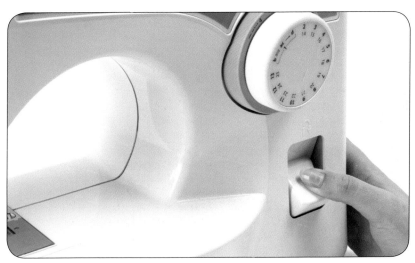

ABOVE If you depress the reverse button on a sewing machine while stitching, the fabric will change direction as it feeds under the needle.

Question 73:
What is tacking stitch?

Tacking stitch is a temporary stitch used to hold two or more layers together that may be removed later on, or stitched down permanently at a normal stitch length. Tacking can be done by hand (see Question 67) or by machine.

To machine tack, set your stitch length on the largest number (4.0 or higher) and do not backstitch (see Question 72). It is advisable to use machine tacking when sewing together your test garment – the stitches can then be removed easily if you need to make adjustments to the fit.

If you are working with multiple layers, tack first, so that layers don't slip when you sew them permanently by machine. Other uses for tacking include pleats, trims, pockets or gathering stitches.

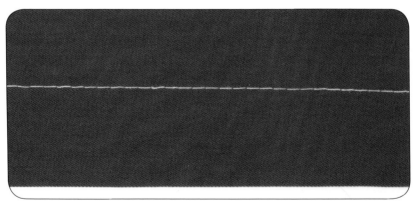

ABOVE Machine tacking is done with the longest stitch length possible. Longer stitches will be easier to remove when you come to take out the tacking.

Question 74:
My stitches are skipping; what should I do?

Skipped stitches usually mean there's a problem with your needle. Be sure that you are using the right size and type of needle for your fabric. Lighter weight fabrics require a smaller size needle.

You should also check that your needle is correctly inserted. Machine needles have a small groove, known as a scarf, located just above the eye. This indentation must be facing a certain direction to create smooth, even stitches. On most machines, it should face toward the back but you should consult the manual to verify the correct way to insert needles on your machine.

Sewing machine needles get bent or blunt at the tip – often caused by

hitting a pin while sewing. Ideally, they should be replaced at the end of every project.

Finally, skipped stitches sometimes occur when the bobbin thread is not the same type as the top or spool thread. Try rewinding the bobbin with the spool thread you are currently using.

EXPERT TIP

66 Do not wind thread on your bobbin over existing thread. Always wind thread on a clean, empty bobbin to keep the tension accurate. 99

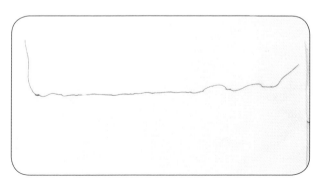

LEFT If you have a problem with skipped stitches, remove the stitching, change the needle and then sew the seam or hem again.

Question 75:
My stitches are loose on top; what's wrong?

Loose threads on the top of your seam usually mean that the tension of your upper thread is not set correctly. Generally speaking, the tension dial is located along the top of your machine with a range of settings, usually from 1 to 9: a higher number means a tighter stitch or tighter tension.

For most types of fabrics, the dial should be set in the middle, between 4 and 6. (Sometimes the dial gets accidentally moved if you bump against it). The thread has to pass snugly between the tension discs so it will feed through the machine properly. Since you can't see the tension discs, the best way to correct this is to rethread your upper thread and adjust the tension slightly. If you are still having trouble, change the needle and check to see that the bobbin is also threaded correctly and that the thread is wound tightly (not loosely) on the bobbin.

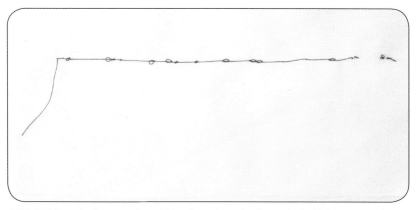

ABOVE When the bottom thread (the thread coming from the bobbin), appears in loops on the top of your sewing, the top, spool thread is probably too tight.

Question 76:
There are lots of tangled threads on the bottom of my fabric; how do I correct this?

If this happens, the tension on the top thread is not correct, causing the stitches to form loosely instead of snugly on the bottom side of your fabric. To correct this, rethread the upper thread, making sure you have inserted the thread properly in the take-up lever (the hook at the upper right of your machine that raises up when the needle raises up).

On some machines, the presser foot must be in the up position when you thread the machine so that the thread then passes through the take-up lever and the tension discs properly.

You may also need to oil your bobbin case so the thread passes through it smoothly. Check your owner's manual for instructions on how to oil your machine properly.

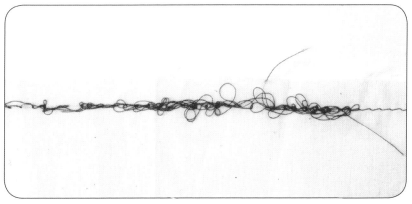

ABOVE When you can see long loops of your top, spool thread on the underside of your sewing, the top thread is either wrongly threaded or the tension is too loose.

Question 77:
How do I keep the seam from puckering?

Puckered seams look as if the threads are too snug or beginning to gather up, rather than lying flat and smooth. First check the needle size to be sure it is a good match to your fabric. Sheer or fine fabrics require a smaller size needle (60/8 or 65/9). Synthetic fabrics such as polyester or nylon are more likely to pucker than natural fibres like cotton, silk, or wool. Pressing seams after sewing also helps smooth out puckering.

If you are still having trouble, try this: hold the fabric behind and in front of the needle as you sew, but don't pull on the fabric – just hold it taut. The fabric must be held at the same amount of tension with both hands as the fabric moves through the machine; if you pull the fabric too much from the back, you may bend or break the needle. This method is called taut stitching.

ABOVE Holding the fabric taut in the sewing machine can help prevent your seams puckering as you stitch.

Question 78:
My machine is stuck and won't sew; what do I do?

Occasionally, your sewing machine can seize up and the fabric won't move backwards or forwards. This can occur at both the start of a seam and in the middle of stitching. To start with, you may have to jiggle the hand wheel a little, to free the needle. After raising the needle and the presser foot, extract the fabric. Sometimes, you can find the thread all tangled up underneath and so the fabric is caught in the machine; use a seam ripper or small scissors to cut the threads. Unpick any untidy stitching.

After taking out the fabric, rethread both the top and bottom threads, and begin again in this order: place the fabric under the presser foot (check the alignment of the raw edge against the seam guides on the throat plate) and turn the hand wheel towards you so the needle pierces the fabric; then put the presser foot in the down position and begin stitching.

When you reach the end of the seam, raise the needle to its highest position by turning the hand wheel again, towards you. Always start and stop sewing with the needle in the highest position.

EXPERT TIP

66 Thread that splits can also cause your sewing machine to jam, so avoid this by using a good quality thread. Using the same thread top and bottom also reduces jamming. 99

5
SEAMS, DARTS AND HEMS

Question 79:
What is a seam allowance?

A seam allowance is the distance between the stitch line and the edge of the fabric when you sew together two or more layers of fabric. The correct amount of seam allowance is included in most commercial patterns, so that when you cut out your pattern you have incorporated the extra fabric you need to create the seam allowances around the edge of each piece.

How do you know where to stitch so as to have the right amount of seam allowance? Your sewing machine has a series of lines on the throat plate to the right of your needle that mark a distance from the needle. They often include both metric and imperial measurements and can range from 1cm to 2.5cm, and ⅛in to 1in. By lining up the edge of your fabric with these marks as you sew, you will be able to keep the distance from the stitching to the edge of the fabric even.

Most commercial patterns are drafted with a 1.5cm (⅝in) seam allowance, but check the guide sheet to confirm this. Patterns designed for knits may have a smaller seam allowance, such as 1cm (⅜in), but again check your pattern guide sheet.

LEFT The seam allowance is the distance between your line of stitching and the raw edge of the fabric. It's essential to keep to the recommended allowance; if you deviate from the correct allowance you could compromise the fit of your garment.

Question 80:
How do I keep my stitch lines straight?

Straight stitching comes with practice, but there are several tricks you can use to sew straight seams. When sewing a seam, keep your eye on the guidelines on the throat plate (see Question 79), rather than on the needle or even the stitches. You can also place a piece of sticky tape on the bed of your sewing machine and keep the edge of your fabric aligned with this as you sew.

When you need to sew a straight line – such as topstitching – in the middle of the garment, the guidelines on the throat plate will be covered up. To help you stitch straight in this instance, draw a line with tailor's chalk and a ruler where you want to sew. Alternatively, place a strip of sticky tape on the fabric along the line you want to sew and use the edge of the tape as a guide. You can also use the edge of your presser foot as a guide for stitching small widths.

ABOVE The throat plate is the metal plate under the needle on your sewing machine. Stitching guides are marked on the throat plate to the right of the needle.

Question 81:
How do I press seams?

It is important to press seams throughout the sewing process, as this helps your garments to look neater and more professional. To press a seam, first open it out, wrong side up and lay on the ironing board. Then press it open and flat with the point of the iron, from start to finish. Make sure the iron is on the correct temperature setting for your fabric; use a pressing cloth if necessary.

A curved seam is a little harder to manipulate on a flat surface such as an ironing board, so place it over a tailor's ham, wrong side of the garment facing up, and press the seam open on the ham.

Sometimes, you will need to press both seam allowances to one side; for example, if you were to topstitch over the seam, or if you need to press a neck seam toward a collar piece. Sometimes your guide sheet will illustrate in which direction to press a seam, but with practice, you will know how to do this for the best-looking results on the front of the garment.

ABOVE To press a seam open, lay it out, wrong side of the garment up, and run the tip of your iron along the seam, between the two allowances.

Question 82:
How do I stitch a curved seam?

A curved seam joins two pieces that are curved either inward or outward. A round neckline with a facing is an example of an inward curve, and a shirt collar with rounded points is an example of an outward curve. Both are enclosed seams, which means they are hidden once they are turned.

Start by stay stitching each curve first (see Question 71). Pin the edges together, matching notches; place the pins in the fabric perpendicular to the edge so you can pull them out easily as you sew. As you sew, turn the curve to keep the raw edge aligned with the stitch guide on your throat plate. When finished, clip the seam as described in Question 83. After clipping, turn the seam to the outside, under-stitch (see Question 121) and press.

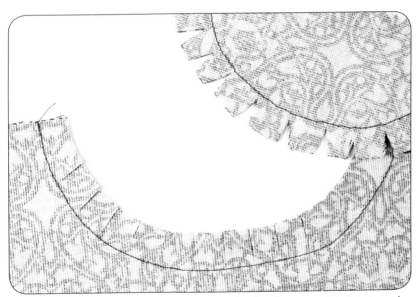

ABOVE After stitching curved seams you must clip the allowances. Snip into inward curving seams (bottom) and cut small triangles out of outward curving seams (top).

Question 83:
What does it mean to trim, clip and grade a seam?

There are three techniques applied to an enclosed seam (rather than an exposed one) to help it lie flat, reduce bulk and look smooth on the outside of the garment. To trim a seam means that you cut the seam allowance to make it narrower after you have sewn it: a 1.5cm (⅝in) stitched seam is trimmed to 1cm

(⅜in). This can be done on a curved or straight seam. Only curved seams need clipping and to do this you cut into the seam allowance from the raw edge to the stitch line at 12mm (½in) intervals. This helps 'release' the curve so the seam lays flat when turned to the inside of the garment. Grading a seam is similar to

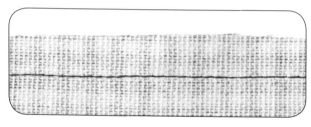

LEFT This seam has been trimmed: the width of both seam allowances has been reduced.

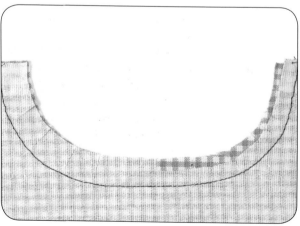

LEFT The left-hand side of this curved seam has been clipped. The right hand side has been clipped and then graded – the width of one seam allowance only has been reduced.

Seams, Darts and Hems

trimming but just one of the seam allowances is reduced in depth. This helps prevent the edges of the seam forming a ridge on the outside.

Some or all of these steps may be applied to enclosed seams but how do you decide which is required? It depends on the fabric, where the seam is located on the garment, and if you plan to add anything to the finished edge, like a trim or topstitching. A curved seam should always be clipped. Any seam that looks bulky should be graded. If you topstitch the edge, trimming is a good idea. You can try one method and see how it looks – if the seam looks unsatisfactory on the outside after you press, try another of these steps until the seam looks flat and smooth on the outside.

Question 84:
How do I pin and sew a dart?

A dart is a fold of fabric sewn into the garment to create shape. They are placed at areas of the body that are curved, such as the bust, waist, shoulder or elbow. Although there are many types of darts, they all require accurate marking, stitching and pressing. (See Question 56 for marking darts.)

To stitch a dart, first fold the dart down the middle on the wrong side of the fabric, matching the two dotted lines that form the dart; pin in place. To sew, begin at the wide end (the dart base) and backstitch (see Question 72). Continue sewing along the dart line to the other end (called the point).

If using a thin or sheer fabric, do not backstitch at the point, as this can cause the dart to 'bunch up' in your sewing machine. It can also show on the outside of the garment. Instead, leave long tails of thread and secure the ends by tying them together. When sewing with a fabric you have not used before, always sew a test sample first.

Question 85:
How do I pin and sew a princess seam?

A princess seam runs vertically down the centre of the bust line, from either the shoulder or the armhole, to create shape. If your garment's bodice is made up of front and side-front pieces you will get a princess seam when you stitch together the opposing curves of the front and side fronts. A princess seam is not the same as a curved seam described in Question 82, where the two edges are the same shape; one edge is curved inward and one is curved outward. Getting them to line up properly requires that you clip seam allowances before you pin and sew together.

Stay-stitch (see Question 71) the curve of the front piece 1cm (³⁄₈in) inside the seam line. Clip every 1cm (³⁄₈in) (see Question 83) around the curve to release it. Pin the curved edge to the side-front piece, matching notches – because

you've already clipped into the seam allowance of the front piece, its curve will 'bend' around the curve of the side-front piece. Stitch with a normal stitch length and seam allowance (not forgetting to backstitch). It's best to sew with the side front facing down and the clipped edge facing up. If you have trouble fitting the two curves together, clip more frequently along the front curve.

ABOVE Clipping the seam allowance makes it easier to press the seam flat.

ABOVE Clip the curve of the front edge before pinning to the side-front.

Question 86:
How do I press darts and princess seams?

Both darts and princess seams create the shape of your garment in curved areas, such as the bust, so it is important to press them correctly once you have stitched the seam. A tailor's ham is the best tool to use (see Question 8). To press a dart, lay it on the tailor's ham, inside facing up. Smooth the dart over the ham so it lies flat and smooth, then press over the dart. Make sure there are no folds or creases as you press. Use a press cloth to avoid over-pressing, which can cause the line of the dart fold to 'shine' through on the outside of the garment. Let the garment cool before removing it from the tailor's ham. The dart should 'puff' up a bit when you turn it to the right side, because you are adding shape to that area.

To press a princess seam, place it over the ham seam-side up and press the seam open. Then press again with the allowances facing the front piece, so the clips are hidden underneath. You can also leave the seam pressed open and clip the other seam allowance if needed for it to lie flat. This depends on the fabric; a fine fabric will look best if the allowances are pressed to one side, but a thicker fabric, or garment that will be lined, may look better with an open seam. For lined garments, press the garment seams open and the lining seams to one side to reduce bulk.

ABOVE A piece of card placed under a dart prevents marks on the right side.

EXPERT TIP

❝ When pressing a dart, place a small strip of thin cardboard between the dart and the garment before you press. This helps prevent the fold from showing on the right side of the garment. ❞

Question 87:

My dart looks bulky; how do I make it lie flat?

Sometimes a dart that is rather wide can look bulky on the right side of the garment, even if you have pressed it correctly. This usually occurs with a full bust. To make the dart look smoother, slash through the middle of it along the fold and press it open, like a seam. Trim the edges of the dart if it appears to be too wide.

You can also overlock the edges once you cut the dart open, but before doing this, test sew and press. Sometimes overlocking stitches show through to the right side of the garment when pressed on a thin or sheer fabric; following the Tip with Question 86 can help avoid this problem.

The point of a dart can look bubbly or too sharp if it has not been stitched smoothly at the tip. If your dart looks like this, re-sew from halfway along the dart toward the tip and straighten the stitch line so it is close to the folded edge – avoid a wide stitch close to the tip. The closer you stitch to the fold as you near the point, the smoother it will look on the right side.

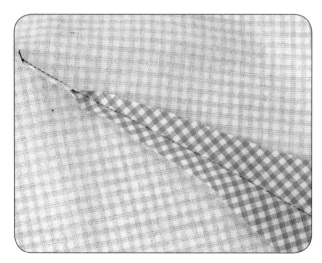

LEFT If you slash along a dart on the wrong side of the garment, you can press it open, like a seam, so that it lies flat.

Question 88:
How do I keep the raw edges of the fabric from unravelling?

Some fabrics have a tendency to unravel at the cut edges more than others, but there are several methods you can use to minimise or hide this. If you own an overlocker, use the three thread option to finish the fabric edges, whether open or closed. If you do not have access to an overlocker, you can cut the edges with pinking shears. For both of these methods, it is best to cut just the edge of the seam, rather than cut too close to the stitch line. It is also better to trim your edges after you have sewn the seam, instead of before, in case you have to change the seam to adjust fit. You can also use your machine's zigzag stitch to finish raw edges.

However, if your fabric unravels a lot even before you begin to assemble the garment, you may want to finish all the edges of each piece before you begin sewing. This does take a bit of time and you may have to do finish the edges again if you change the seam size later on.

You could also consider a French seam. This finished seam requires an extra stitch step, but it does hide the seam edges completely on the inside (see Question 89).

ABOVE Pinking the edge of fabric can help prevent unravelling. You can also run a line of stay stitching along the edge for greater security.

Question 89:
What is a French seam?

A French seam is a narrow, enclosed seam that hides the raw edges on the inside of the seam. It looks like a regular seam on the outside. Sewn on straight rather than curved edges, a French seam is most often used on sheer fabrics because the seam looks neat on both the inside and outside of the garment.

To sew a French seam, place wrong sides of the fabric together and stitch a 6mm (¼in) seam. Trim the seam by another 3mm (⅛in). Press the seam to one side, then fold along the seam so the right sides face each other. Press and pin in place. Sew the seam again, 1cm (⅜in) from the folded edge. The second line of stitching must completely enclose the raw edges of the first seam. Press the seam to one side.

LEFT After sewing the first part of a French seam, fold the seam right sides together and stitch the seam again.

Question 90:
What is a Hong Kong seam finish?

A Hong Kong finish covers the raw edge of a seam with a strip of fabric that's been cut on the bias. It's a great option for an unlined or partially lined garment because it creates a clean, professional look on the inside. The bias binding should be made with a lightweight fabric – such as silk charmeuse or organza – so it does not add bulk to the seams. You can cover each seam allowance separately – an open seam – or both allowances together – a closed seam.

To bind an open seam, you need two bias strips, each as long as the seam and 2.5cm (1in) wide; for a closed seam you need one 2.5cm (1in) wide strip as long as the seam. For an open seam, first press the seam open. Pin the bias strip to one side of the seam allowance, right sides together, and stitch, leaving a 6mm (¼in) seam allowance at the seam edge. Avoid stretching the bias strip as you sew. Press the seam open again, pressing the bias strip flat and to the side. Then turn the strip to the underside of the seam so it wraps around the raw edge; press and pin. Sew again in the seam line (also known as 'stitch in the ditch'). Trim off excess binding if it extends past the original stitch line of the seam. Repeat with the other side of the seam allowance. You can use the same technique for a closed seam, but don't press the seam open and keep both allowances together when you sew on the bias strip.

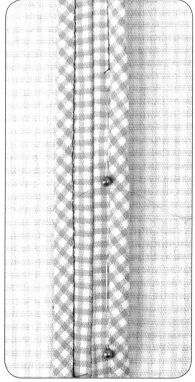

ABOVE On a Hong Kong finish, bias strips are stitched around the raw edges.

Question 91:
What is a flat-felled seam?

A flat-felled seam is characterised by two rows of stitches along a seam that are visible on the outside of a garment. This type of seam is usually found in the side seam of jeans, but they also appear in other casual garments such as skirts, unlined jackets and sportswear.

To create a flat-felled seam, sew a normal seam and press the seam allowances to one side. Then trim the bottom seam allowance to 6mm (¼in) width. Wrap the uncut (upper) seam allowance around the trimmed seam allowance and tuck or fold it underneath it to cover the raw edge completely. Press again and then stitch the seam down, close to the folded edge. The seam on the outside will look almost identical to the seam on the inside.

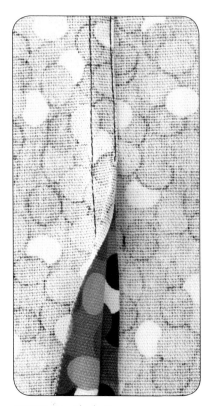

ABOVE Trim the bottom seam allowance, then wrap the wider upper allowance around it and stitch down.

Question 92:
What is a welt seam?

A welt seam looks similar to a flat-felled seam on the outside, but the stitch steps are slightly different. To stitch a welt seam, sew a normal seam and press the seam allowances to one side. You can finish the edges with an overlocker, a zigzag stitch or pinking shears. Turn the garment to the right side and stitch along the allowances 6–10mm (¼–³⁄₈in) from the seam line. Since you are sewing in the middle of the garment, you will not have the advantage of the seam guides on the throat plate to help stitch a straight line. Instead, align the edge of the presser foot to the seam line as you sew to create a straight line.

A welt seam is also sometimes referred to as a topstitched seam. It can be used around the edges of pockets, collars, cuffs, or on any seam to add a decorative element. You could try using a contrasting thread to turn this seam finish into a design detail.

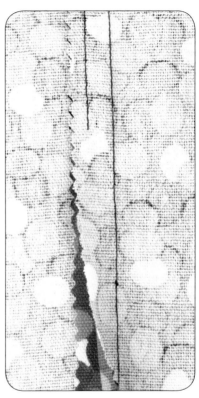

ABOVE Finish the raw edges then press the seam to one side before stitching through all the layers.

Question 93:
What is a clean-edge finish?

A clean-edge finish (also known as 'turned-and-stitched') gives a neater look and helps to prevent fraying during washing and wear. It works best on a straight seam and requires extra rows of stitching once the seam is sewn.

To apply a clean-edge finish, first press the seam open and flat. Then turn under the edge of one seam allowance by 3mm (⅛in) and press. Stitch along the edge of the allowance, close to the fold, so that it is stitched down. Repeat for the other seam edge.

A clean-edge finish is best for light- to medium-weight fabrics. It may look bulky in thicker fabrics and it can be difficult to fold under seam edges by 3mm (⅛in) if the fabric is textured, such as a bouclé or tweed. The best finish to use on any seam is determined by the weight and type of fabric.

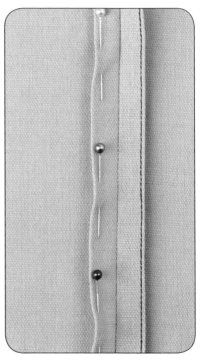

ABOVE After pressing the seam open, turn under the raw edges and press. Pin and then stitch in place.

Question 94:
What is topstitching?

Topstitching is one or more straight rows of stitching sewn on the right side of a garment. It is often seen in casual garments and works best on medium-weight fabrics, rather than fine or sheer fabrics. When topstitching, always sew on the outside of the garment so you have more control over how accurately you sew.

Before you begin, make sure the area you are topstitching is pressed flat and positioned just where you want it, since a topstitch shows on the outside of a garment and draws attention to the area where it is applied. The area you want to topstitch may be located in the middle of the garment, so you won't be able to see the stitching guides on the throat plate. In this case, use the edge of your presser foot as a guide along the edge you are sewing. If the location of the stitch line is wider than the presser foot, apply sticky tape along the line you want to sew and use that as a guide next to your presser foot edge.

Most topstitching, however, goes right next to an edge or a seam, so you have a built-in guide to follow for even stitching. You can also use one of the decorative stitch options on your machine as a topstitch.

EXPERT TIP

66 A double needle allows you to sew two rows of stitches at the same time and guarantee that they will be parallel. The shaft or upper half of the needle fits most sewing machines while the lower half splits into two separate needles. You need two spools of thread and one bobbin. To thread, hold the two spool threads like one strand and thread through the sewing maching normally before splitting and threading the two needles. The bobbin is threaded as usual. This type of needle does not turn corners very well, but does work on straight or slightly curved edges. 99

Question 95:
Where can I apply topstitching?

Topstitching can be decorative or functional, depending on where you apply it and the look you want to create in your garment. You can use it to decorate a garment by topstitching one or two rows parallel to the edge of a collar, say, or a cuff or yoke. Topstitch along the edge of a side seam or shoulder seam to create a more casual look. To add interest, use a contrasting thread colour.

Topstitching can be functional too: it can strengthen a seam. Work it along a seam, right side up and close to the original seam line, after it has been pressed flat. Topstitching is also an ideal way to sew down the edge of a waistband to hold it in place. When used to stitch down shirt pockets or along the opening of a side-seam pocket it can be both decorative and functional.

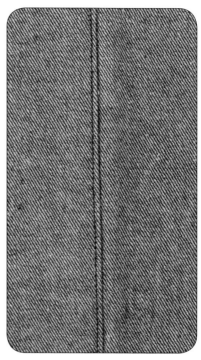

ABOVE A line of topstitching can add strength to a seam and reinforces seams on hard-wearing fabrics.

Question 96:
How do I stitch knit fabrics?

Because knit fabrics are stretchy, the seams should be constructed so that they also have some give in them; this is to prevent the thread from breaking when the garment is stretched during wear. Polyester thread (usually labelled as all-purpose) is a good choice for knits because it is strong and elastic. A ballpoint needle is also useful because it passes between the yarns of a knit (rather than piercing them) which helps prevent damaging the fabric as you sew.

Some sewing machines have a stretch-stitch option, which automatically backstitches at regular intervals as you sew, to create some give in the seam. You can also use a narrow zigzag stitch; use a shorter stitch length to reduce thread breakage. Try pulling gently on the seam behind the presser foot as you sew to add a bit of give. It's a good idea to experiment with these options on a scrap of fabric before sewing together the garment.

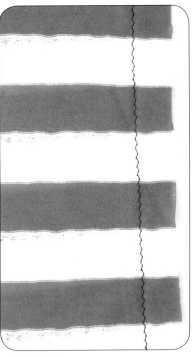

ABOVE A zigzag stitch has more give in it than a straight stitch, making it more suitable for seams in stretchy knits.

Question 97:
How do I stitch slippery or delicate fabrics?

Sheer fabric such as chiffon, silk charmeuse, or any lightweight fabric can be tricky to sew and frustrating without a few tips to help the process. To start with, fit your machine with a fine needle (size 8, 9, or 10) and test on a sample before sewing the seams. If the seams pucker, loosen the tension dial.

To keep the fabric layers in place as you sew, place a piece of tissue paper under the garment when you put it in the sewing machine and stitch through the fabric and tissue. The paper gives your sewing machine's feed something firm to grab onto. You can place tissue on top as well, if the fabric still slips. The paper tears off easily afterwards. When you sew the seam, start and stop stitching about 12mm (½in) from the ends to avoid bunching of the fabric.

You can also hand sew certain parts of the garments, such as the darts, before stitching permanently. Seams can also be hand tacked before permanent stitching – it doesn't take that long and will save the tearing out of stitches later on.

LEFT Place tissue paper under your fabric when you stitch sheers. The feed teeth in your machine's throat plate will grip on the paper rather than the delicate fabric.

Question 98:
How do I turn up and pin a hem by myself?

When you've sewn together a garment and are ready to do the hem, try it on and stand in front of a full-length mirror. Pin up the hem at the centre front, sides and centre back; it's awkward, but pin it once for now. Take off the garment and lie it out flat, inside out, with the side seams touching – that is, fold the garment in half at the centre front and centre back. Pin up the rest of the hem between the four points you've already pinned, lining up the two layers.

Try the garment on again and make adjustments until the hem looks even on all sides. Look in the mirror sideways to be sure the hem hangs evenly front to back. Use a hand mirror to help you see the rear view. Press the hem flat, then trim all but 4cm (1½in) off the edge. For skirts or dresses with a full curved edge, let the garment hang on a coat hanger for 24–48 hours prior to hemming in case it stretches.

EXPERT TIP

66 If you are hemming a skirt that is part of a two-piece suit, put on the jacket while you pin up the hem. Wearing both pieces will help you pin up a hem that's the right proportion for the whole ensemble. Remember to wear your usual outdoor shoes as well. 99

Question 99:
How do I mark the hem edge?

Once you have determined the correct hem length and it has been pinned in place, the next step is to mark and trim the hem allowance.

To mark the hem edge, slide the garment, inside out, over the narrow end of the ironing board so that a single layer lays flat on the board. Press the folded edge down. Then remove the pins and unfold the hem. Determine the amount of hem allowance you need. (see Question 100). With your seam gauge, measure and mark that amount every few inches, below the crease around the perimeter of the hem. Cut along the line created by the markings to remove excess fabric. When you measure, be sure to include an additional 12mm (½in) if you are going to turn the raw edge under before sewing the hem.

ABOVE You can use your seam gauge to check you are pinning up your hem to the correct depth after trimming off the excess fabric.

Question 100:
How wide should the hem allowance be?

The hem allowance is the extra amount of fabric added below the finished edge of your garment. The width of the allowance depends on the shape of the garment and the fabric's weight and drape. A straight garment, such as a pencil skirt, requires a wider hem allowance for a dressier look and to add support to the garment. A full garment that has a curved edge works best with a narrow hem.

A skirt or dress hem should measure 12–50mm (½–2in). Whether you sew by hand or machine, this amount adds structure and support to the finished garment. It also looks better on dressier garments. The circumference of the hem allowance must be the same as the finished hem line on the garment so that it will lay flat and smooth when stitched down. The circumference of a curved hem changes as you move up the width of the skirt, so the hem must be narrow to lay flat against the curve.

EXPERT TIP

❝ All pattern pieces include a hem allowance, but you may wish to add length to each piece when you cut your fabric, just in case you need it later on. You can always cut the extra amount off after your final fitting. ❞

Question 101:
Do I need to use hem tape?

Hem tape is a length of tape which is stitched to the hem allowance; the edge of the tape is then stitched to the garment. You can use a woven-fabric tape or a lace tape. (These differ from iron-on hemming tape, a fusible webbing which is used for no-sew, easy hems.)

A woven tape works best on a straight hem for medium weight fabrics because the firm weave lays flat against the garment and provides a secure fabric to stitch on. The lace tape is more suitable for curved hems because it has a bit of give so you can ease it around the hem as you sew. Hem tape helps reduce bulk, controls fraying and adds a decorative touch to the inside of the garment.

ABOVE Hem tape is stitched to the raw edge of the hem allowance and then hemmed to the garment.

Question 102:
How do I sew a hem by hand?

Knowing how to hand sew hems is an important dressmaking skill, even though most hems in shop-bought clothes are machine stitched. Whatever method you use, your hem should be done with care and accuracy, as it is one of the most visible aspects of a garment.

Before you begin, finish the raw edge of the hem by one of these methods: serge, turn under and machine stitch, cut with pinking shears, or apply hem tape. Then turn under the hem by the required amount and press. Thread your sewing needle with a 45cm (18in) length of thread and tie a simple knot at the end. Turn the garment to the inside and secure the thread in the hem allowance.

One stitch to use is catch stitch. If you are right-handed, hold the needle parallel to the hem, pointing to the left, and move right as you stitch. (Simply reverse this if you are left-handed.) Pick up two to three fabric strands on the hem allowance with the needle and then pull the sewing thread through completely. Move to the right 12mm (½in), and cross over and pick up just one fabric strand on the garment side; pull the needle through completely. Keep the stitches close to the hem edge. Again, move to the right 12mm (½in), cross over to the hem side, and pick up two to three

fabric strands. Continue stitching in the same way until the hem is completed; tie off with a simple knot close to the fabric. The stitches will cross back and forth between the garment and the hem allowance. This type of hem is nearly invisible on the outside when done properly.

For hem stitch (also known as slip stitch), follow the steps above to prepare the hem edge, needle and garment. Hold the needle as for catch stitch, but for this hem, you will move in the same direction the needle is pointing – to the left if you are right-handed, to the right if left-handed. Pick up two to three fabric strands on the hem side, move left 12mm (½in) and pick up just one strand on the garment side. Pull the thread through completely and continue in the same way until done. Tie off near the fabric. This hem is a bit faster and more suitable for fabrics that are not bulky.

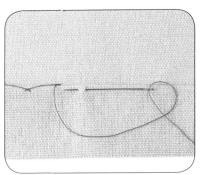

ABOVE Catch stitch is worked in the direction that the needle eye points.

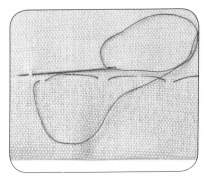

ABOVE Hem stitch is worked in the same direction as the needle point.

Question 103:
How do I machine stitch a hem?

Sewing a hem by machine is the quickest way to finish a hem, but because a machine-stitched hem is more-or-less permanent, be sure you prepare the hem accurately first: measure, trim, pin and press (see Questions 98 to 100). If you make a mistake and have to rip out the stitches, it doesn't save you any time in the end!

To sew by machine, turn under the raw edge of the hem allowance 12mm (½in) and press flat. Pin the hem down with the pins perpendicular to the edge (so you can pull them out easily as you sew). Stitch along the upper fold (where you turned the raw edge). Start and stop your stitches in a seam so the backstitches are not as noticeable.

A hem that is stitched 2.5cm (1in) above the bottom looks best for casual garments such as tops, T-shirts, sundresses and sportswear. To add interest, sew another row of stitches along the bottom edge of the hem – see Question 94 for topstitching directions.

EXPERT TIP

❝ Instead of using a plain, straight stitch around the hem, you could add interest with a decorative machine stitch. Before you do, it is advisable to machine or hand tack the hem in place first. ❞

LEFT Machine-hemming will be visible on the right side of a garment. You could make a feature of this and add topstitching close to the bottom of the hem.

Question 104:
My machine has a blind hem feature; how do I use it?

A blind hemstitch is a wonderful feature on a sewing machine, allowing you to stitch hems that are nearly invisible on the right side of a garment. If your machine has this, it will also include a special foot, although you can also sew a blind hem with a standard foot. It is easy to use, but the key to success is the way you fold the hem before sewing.

A blind hem features a pattern of three or four straight stitches and one zigzag stitch, repeated the entire edge of the hem. The zigzag catches just a thread or two on the garment side, while the straight stitches sew along the fold of the hem's raw edge.

To prepare the hem, turn the hem allowance to the inside and press. Then turn under the raw edge of the hem allowance and press again. To sew, lay the hem, wrong side facing up, on the bed of your machine. Fold the hem allowance toward the garment right side, keeping the folded raw edge exposed by about 6mm (¼in). Slide the fold under your presser foot and line up the needle so the straight stitches of the blind hem sew the raw edge fold and the zigzag catches the left fold.

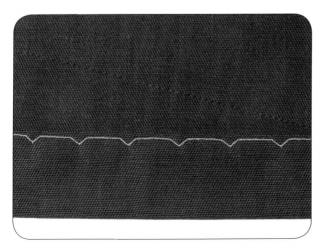

LEFT A blind hemstitch is a useful feature on a sewing machine. It allows you to machine stitch hems that are more akin to hand-stitched hems.

Question 105:
How do I turn up and sew a curved, full hem edge?

A hem that is full and curved can be stitched either by hand or machine, but it must be prepared differently to a straight hem because the width at the edge is different from the width at the hem fold.

Measure a hem allowance of 12–25mm (½–1in). Finish the raw edge of the hem allowance with an overlocker, with pinking shears, or with zigzag stitching close to the edge. Machine tack 6mm (¼in) from the finished edge around the entire hem. Draw up the tacking so that the width of the edge matches the width of the garment when turned up. Pin and press in place, then sew by machine or by hand.

While a machine-stitched hem is quicker, a hand-stitched hem may be preferable for a dressy garment or to achieve more a couture look. Hand sewing gives you more control over the stitches (especially with a slippery fabric) and you can make the stitches nearly invisible.

EXPERT TIP

❝ To help distribute the ease evenly, pin up first at the side seams or at regular intervals, then fill in the rest with pins. ❞

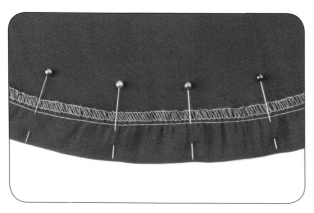

LEFT A line of machine tacking worked just below the finished edge of a curved hem, allows you to gather up the fabric fullness when pinning in place.

Question 106:
What is a rolled hem edge?

A rolled or narrow rolled hem refers to a type of hand-stitched hem that is very narrow and almost invisible. It is ideal for lightweight and sheer fabrics and works best when you use good quality thread and a sharp, small needle.

To create a rolled hem, add a 12mm (½in) hem allowance to the finished hem measurement. Stay stitch 12mm (½in) from the cut edge of the hem allowance. Fold under and press along the stitching. Trim the hem to 6mm (¼in) and turn the hem under again. Hand sew,

catching just one or two threads on the garment side. Trim a few inches of hem allowance at a time. Use the point of the needle to tuck the hem under as you sew.

A rolled hem can also be done by machine (although the stitches show on the outside) with a special presser foot. The foot automatically turns or rolls the raw edge of the fabric as it feeds into the machine just before it is stitched down. With a bit of practice, this technique can be mastered for sewing narrow hems by machine.

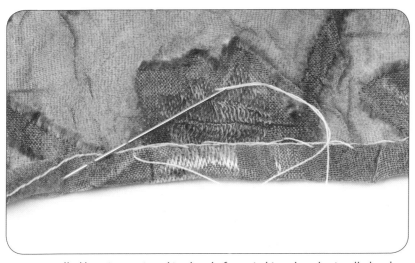

ABOVE A rolled hem is not pinned in place before stitching; the edge is rolled under as you stitch by hand.

6
INTERFACINGS AND LININGS

Question 107:
What is interfacing?

Interfacing is a fabric sewn on the inside of a garment to support, stabilise and retain the shape of certain sections. It is made from a variety of fabric types and weights, and usually comes in white, black and grey. The type of interfacing you choose depends on your fabric as well as the section of garment to which it is attached. The most common locations for interfacing are collars, cuffs, facings, lapels, pocket flaps, openings, closures or any area of the garment that needs more stability than the fabric itself gives. It is always applied to the wrong side of the garment.

You may use several types of different interfacings within the same garment, if the support you need varies from one section to another. For example, a tailored shirt-dress may require a medium-weight interfacing for its notched collar, and a more lightweight interfacing for the sleeve hem.

LEFT Interfacing is a special type of fabric and comes in white, grey and black. It ranges in weight from ultra light (for sheers) through to heavy (for thick fabrics).

EXPERT TIP

❝ As you become familiar with the use of interfacing, you may find it has many more uses than that recommended your pattern guide sheet. It makes a great stabiliser in zip seams, or behind appliqués and rows of decorative stitching. ❞

Question 108:
What type of interfacing should I buy?

Since there are so many varieties of interfacing, it is easy to get confused when you try to select the right one for your project. There are three major types in interfacing: woven, which looks like fabric with lengthwise and crosswise threads; non-woven, which is made of bonded material, has no visible grain lines, and does not unravel; and knit, which has a slight give, is more flexible and lightweight, and looks like tricot or lingerie fabric.

Each of these interfacing types also comes in a variety of fibre contents and weights. Colours include white, off white, black and grey. Interfacings are either fusible (iron-on) or non fusible (sew-in). Fusible interfacing is popular because it saves stitching time and, once ironed in place, it stays put. Non-fusible interfacing is best for sheer fabrics as there is no glue to seep through or distort the fabric. It is also ideal for those fabrics that do not tolerate heat or pressure well,

such as metallic cloth, or napped fabrics like velvet.

Your garment fabric determines the type of interfacing to use but if you are unsure about which weight interfacing to use, err on the side of lightweight. It's better to have a lighter weight of interfacing than a heavy, stiff one. The interfacing should support the fabric, but not change the handle or feel of it too much. To check on what colour interfacing to buy, hold it underneath a sample of your garment fabric to be sure that the interfacing won't change the colour of the fabric on the outside.

EXPERT TIP

66 Always buy extra interfacing so that when you are working on a current or future project, you don't run out of it in the middle of sewing and have to stop! 99

Question 109:
How do I cut the interfacing?

When you cut out your pattern in fabric, cut out your interfacing at the same time. Your pattern guide sheet will give you instructions as to which pieces to cut out of the interfacing, and how many, as well as instructions on how to lay out and cut the interfacing. The layout instructions may appear in a separate section of the guide sheet, so look for it if you cannot find it near the fabric layout guide. Instructions are also printed on the pattern pieces, so look for these on collars, cuffs and facings.

Woven interfacing should be treated the same way as fabric when you come to match up grain lines on the pattern. Since non-woven interfacings are considered to be

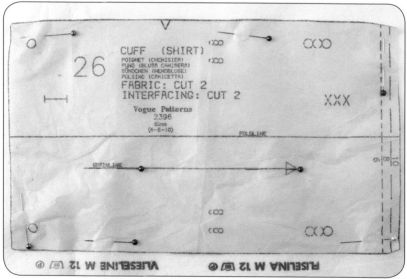

ABOVE When pinning a pattern piece to interfacing, line up the grain lines to the manufactured edge of the interfacing.

bonded fabrics, they do not actually have lengthwise and crosswise grains, however pieces should still be cut according to lengthwise grain for the most stability. Treat the manufactured edge as the lengthwise grain. Knit interfacing should also be cut according to the guide sheet or in the same direction as the garment pieces.

EXPERT TIP

66 For pattern pieces that say 'cut 2', fold the interfacing in half as you would when cutting fabric. This will ensure that you cut mirror images of the pieces and not two left or two right pieces. Interfacing does not always have a noticeable selvage, but the fold should be made parallel to the lengthwise edges as if they were selvages. 99

Question 110:
How do I 'pre-shrink' the interfacing?

Preshrinking your interfacing is a must, just as it is for your fabric. If fusible (iron-on) interfacing is not preshrunk this can cause bubbles to appear on the outside of the garment after washing.

To pre-wash fusible interfacing, fill a sink with hot water and soak the interfacing until the water cools. Hang the interfacing up to dry away from any heat source and out of direct sunlight; do not put it in the dryer! To pre-wash non-fusible (sew-in) interfacing, machine wash and machine or air dry.

If you are in a hurry, the second best way to preshrink is to hold your iron a few inches above the interfacing and apply a few shots of steam – don't let the iron touch fusible interfacing. Let it dry and cool before moving it.

Question 111:
How do I apply fusible interfacing?

Fusible interfacing is applied using pressure, heat, time and moisture. Set your iron to a medium heat. Place the fabric pieces to be interfaced wrong side up on the ironing board. Lay the matching interfacing piece on top with the glue side down, on the wrong side of the fabric. To check which side of the interfacing is the glue side, look closely at it in good light – the glue side will look slightly shiny. If you brush the glue side with your finger tips it will feel rough; this is the side that goes face down against the wrong side of the fabric.

Press down with the iron, using a press cloth and steam if needed. Hold for 10 seconds and do not move the iron back and forth. Lift the iron and check to see if the interfacing adhered to the fabric. If not, repeat the process. Start in the centre and move outward from side to side. Let the piece cool before moving it. It's best to fuse all your pieces at one time, preferably before you begin sewing. That way, you can move through the garment-construction process without interrupting your sewing steps.

EXPERT TIP

❝ Before you go ahead, test your interfacing on a 15cm (6in) square of spare fabric to make sure you like the way it looks and feels with your chosen fabric. ❞

ABOVE Place the fusible interfacing glue-side down on the wrong side of your fabric before pressing.

Question 112:
How do I sew in non-fusible interfacing?

Sew-in interfacing is applied to the wrong side of each interfaced garment piece, just like fusible interfacing. Cut out your pieces of interfacing and then pin to the wrong side of the matching fabric pieces. Hand tack in place, then machine stitch around the edges, just inside the designated seam allowance; for example, if the seam allowance given in the pattern directions is 1.5cm (⅝in), stitch 12mm (½in) in from the raw edge.

If, as you reach the end of your stitching, the interfacing layer wrinkles up, unpick the last edge of stitching, press the fabric and interfacing flat and stitch again. Sometimes the interfacing moves or shifts as you sew around the perimeter, which necessitates the re-stitching step.

If your interfacing is a medium weight or seems to add bulk to the edges, trim off the excess at the seam allowance after you sew. This will reduce bulk inside the seams, especially on collars, cuffs or any other seam that is turned to the inside.

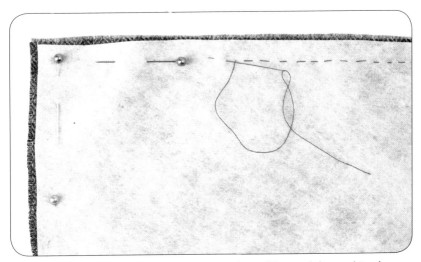

ABOVE Pin your interfacing to the wrong side of your fabric and then tack in place. This helps prevent the interfacing from slipping while you machine stitch.

Question 113:
What type of lining fabric should I use?

Like interfacing, lining fabrics come in a variety of weights, fibre contents and colours. The purpose of a lining is to add comfort, quality and stability to a garment. It also helps the garment slip on and off easily, hides the inner details of the garment and helps the garment hang with smooth flattering lines.

Several factors should be considered when choosing a lining. It should be static free or cling free (check the label on the end of the fabric bolt); the fibre content should be breathable for comfort if worn next to the skin. Silk is an excellent choice for comfort and a silk-lined garment slips on and off easily, however it can be expensive and may not be readily available. Polyester lining is more affordable and available in a variety of colours, but is not as breathable against the skin in warm weather. Rayon lining has a soft feel and and is not as pricey as silk, but it tends to wrinkle. Lightweight cotton, such as batiste, also makes a comfortable lining suitable for lightweight garments.

Lining fabric should always be lighter in weight than the garment fabric and the colour should not show through on the outside of the garment. Woven linings should be used with woven fabrics and knit linings with knit fabrics. Finally, purchase a lining with the same care instructions as the fabric.

You can have fun with linings in jackets, by choosing a contrasting colour or print, as long as it still meets the above criteria. For example, consider a bright pink or teal colour inside a black jacket, or try a paisley print that coordinates with a wool coat fabric.

LEFT There is a wide range of lining fabrics available, in colours to match or contrast with any garment fabric.

Question 114:
What is an 'open' and a 'closed' lining?

If a garment has an open lining it means that the hem edge of the garment and the hem edge of the lining are finished separately, rather than being attached to each other. Since an open lining hangs free from the garment, all seams should be finished on the inside. The lining hem can be machine stitched, but the garment hem should be finished by hand stitching. A lined garment is considered a more tailored or even couture item of clothing and should reflect as much in the final details, such as an invisible hem.

A closed lining is attached to the garment hem and sewn by hand or machine. The seam allowances inside the garment do not need to be finished as the closed lining prevents the inside of the garment from being seen. Both the garment and lining hems can be stitched by hand before the two are sewn together to form the closed lining. The two hems can also be stitched to one another by machine.

All linings should be cut shorter at the hem than the garment to prevent the lining from showing below the garment hem when the garment is finished and being worn. This applies to open and closed linings. The decision of whether to have a closed or open lining depends on the garment style. A closed lining makes a tailored garment more elegant, but may not be suitable for a full skirt. A closed lining requires more accuracy than an open lining, which has the advantage of free movement.

LEFT The lining of a skirt is usually an open lining. The hem of the skirt and the hem of the lining are finished separately and not joined together.

Question 115:
What is the difference between a full and partial lining?

A full lining covers the entire surface of the inside of the garment (except for facings and turned-up hems), whereas a partial lining covers only a portion of the garment, leaving some inner parts of the garment exposed.

A full lining is suitable for jackets, skirts and dresses. A partial lining may be used because some areas of the garment will become too bulky if lined, such as a skirt with a lower pleated edge. The lining may reach from the waist to the top of the pleats, and the pleated area will remain unlined so as not to interfere with the sharpness of the pleats when pressed.

A partial lining may also appear in a man's sport coat (or blazer), where the lower half of the jacket back is left unlined. Specific garment parts, such as a pocket or a collar, may also be partially lined. Choose a partial or full lining carefully as they can affect garment quality and appearance.

ABOVE Jackets usually have a full lining, especially if made from a light- or medium-weight fabric.

Question 116:
Can I add a lining to a unlined garment?

Some garments can be lined easily, even if you don't have separate lining pieces as part of your pattern. You'll get the best results if the garment you want to line is simple and has only a few main pieces; such as a waistcoat, cape, basic jacket with a front opening, or a skirt.

Cut out the lining pieces using the corresponding pattern pieces of the garment. Any fit adjustments you make to a tester garment, must also be made to the lining pieces before sewing them together. Stitch the lining together in the same order as the garment. Press all the lining seams flat. Do not attach any lining to the garment pieces yet. The lining is attached to the garment only at the outer edges.

Put the lining and garment right sides together and stitch around the edges. Leave an opening of about 10cm (4in) – big enough for your hand – in one of the side seams or at the bottom edge. Clip curves and corners as needed. Reach inside between layers through the opening and pull the garment to the outside. Press the edges, then hand stitch the opening closed.

A skirt lining can be joined to the garment at the waistline, before you add the waistband. A waistcoat lining is sewn to the garment along the neckline front and back, and around the armholes, before you sew the side seams.

Garments with sleeves are a bit trickier. Sew the lining to the garment around the neckline edges (but not the armholes). Then sew the sleeves together at the hem and insert the lined sleeves as individual units. The armhole seam will be exposed but you can finish it with a zigzag stitch or bias binding.

Question 117:
Can I omit the lining in a garment?

Although your pattern calls for a lining, you may decide you don't want one. You might be short on time or decide that your garment fabric doesn't need lining – it might feel comfortable next to the skin and doesn't need the ease of lining to help you put it on or take it off. It may also be that combining lining with your chosen fabric could make the garment too warm.

If you decide against a lining then you can leave it off, but there are a few precautions you should take. If the lining in your pattern extends right to the edges of the garment (like the examples described in Question 115), you must add facings to finish the raw edges that would have been covered by lining. To do this you will need to make patterns for new facings (see Questions 127, 162, and 177) and ensure you have enough fabric. You may also wish to finish the raw edges of the seam allowances, since they will be exposed without a lining. See Questions 89 to 93 for some of the seam finishing options available.

Some garments, such as a jacket with a turned collar, include both facings and linings, so if you want to leave out the lining in this case, you need to finish the raw edges of the facings with an overlocker, pinked edge or zigzag stitch.

Question 118:
Do I need a lining with a knit fabric?

Some garments made from a knit fabric will benefit from a lining – this might give a garment more structure, make it more comfortable to wear, or prevent a sheer knit being too see-through. Whether or not to use a lining depends on the fabric, as it does with woven materials.

You can partially line a garment: you might, for example, line the bodice area but leave the sleeves or part of the back unlined. The best option is a flesh-coloured lining that has the same stretch factor as the fabric (think of the lining material

found in swimwear). If you are not sure about using a knit lining, consider buying extra knit fabric and self line – in other words, you should use the same fabric for both lining and garment.

Knit linings should be sewn with the same rules that apply to any knit fabric. Prewash and dry the lining fabric, then sew using a ball-point needle and with your machine set to a zigzag stitch. Remember to stretch the fabric very slightly as it goes through the machine. Always test sew a sample first.

NECKLINES, COLLARS AND POCKETS

Question 119:
How do I sew facing pieces together?

A facing is a piece of fabric sewn to the edges of a garment at the openings to give it support and hide the raw edge. The most common type, a shaped facing, is cut to match the edge to which it is sewn, such as an armhole, neckline, or curved waistband. The facing pieces are interfaced, stitched together and finished around the outer edges before they are attached to the rest of the garment.

To sew the facing pieces together before attaching to your garment, first pin right sides together, matching notches at the short ends. Follow your pattern guide sheet to be sure you are matching edges correctly. For a neckline facing, you stitch together the shoulder seams of the front and back pieces. For armholes, stitch the pieces together at the shoulders and at the underarm or side seam. For waist facings, match the front and back pieces together at the side seams.

EXPERT TIP

66 **If the pieces confuse you, lay them on the section of the garment where they are to be sewn and match corresponding seams.** 99

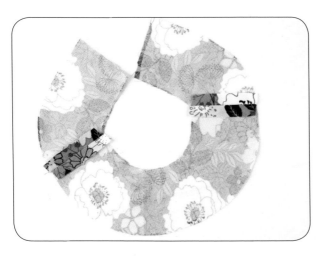

LEFT After interfacing a neckline facing, the pieces are stitched together at the shoulder seams.

Question 120:
How do I sew the facing to the neckline?

Once you have sewn the facing pieces together correctly, the inner edge is sewn to the corresponding edge of the garment. Before you begin, stay stitch around the neckline (see Question 71). Press open the seams on both the garment and the facing. Pin the inner edge of the facing to the neckline, matching the shoulder seams. Stitch around the edge. (See Question 136 on how to sew around a curve, or Question 126 on how to stitch around a corner.)

If the facing looks too big or small as you pin around the edge, check the width of the seam allowance on both the facing and the garment. They should all be the same, according to the pattern guide sheet. If not, re-sew until the edges fit correctly.

After you have sewn the facing to the garment, clip every 12mm (½in) along the seam to open it up so it will turn to the inside of the garment. The next step is to under stitch (see Question 121); this helps the facing stay tucked inside the garment so don't be tempted to skip this step.

LEFT The neck facing is stitched to the garment bodice around the neckline. The seam needs to be clipped before turning the facing to the inside.

Question 121:
What is under stitching?

Under stitching can help prevent a facing from rolling out towards the front of the garment. After sewing the facing to the garment, press the seam allowance toward the facing. Stitch the seam allowances to the facing piece, close to the seam line: do not stitch on the stitch line, but right next to it. Make sure you are sewing the seam allowances to the facing, not to the garment.

Turn the facing to the inside of the garment and press, using your fingers to make sure the facing rolls to the inside. The under stitching should not show on the outside of the garment, but only on the inside, close to the edge.

> ## EXPERT TIP
>
> **66 Under stitching is also good for lined garments where lining edges are sewn to garment edges. The process is the same as for facings and, like the facing application, prevents the lining rolling to the outside. 99**

ABOVE Under stitching should be done on the facing, close to the seam.

Question 122:
How do I make the facing lie flat when I turn it to the inside?

To create a garment with a smooth finish and a professional look it's essential that the facing lies flat.

After you have stitched the facing to the garment (see Question 120), clip the seam every 12mm (½in) from the raw edge to the stitch line. This opens the seam allowance so the facing will turn easily to the inside of the garment. To further reduce bulk, you can grade one seam allowance (see Question 83).

The next step is to under stitch (see Question 121), which helps the facing stay tucked inside the garment. Then turn the facing to the inside and tack the facing down with a few small hand stitches at the seam allowances. Make sure to catch only the seam allowance and not the garment itself. If you want to add a decorative touch, topstitch around the neckline close to the edge, and/or at the outside edge of the facing. The extra stitching also holds the facing in place.

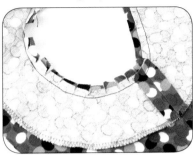

ABOVE Clipping and grading the seam will help a facing lie flat.

Question 123:
The neckline is gaping at the back; how do I fix this?

Sometimes the neckline of a garment sits away from the neck at the back, creating a gap. This often occurs if you have rounded shoulders or a rounded upper back. When you try on the test garment look in the mirror sideways, or get a friend to check the fit at the back of the neck.

If the neckline is gaping, take off the test garment and pin a small dart on either side of the centre back line; adjust these darts until the gap disappears. If your garment has a centre back seam, then you can simply pin the seam deeper at the neck. Stitch along where you have pinned the changes and try on the garment again, making further adjustments if needed. Remember to transfer these changes to your garment pieces when you cut them out. You will also need to change any matching pieces, such as a facing, lining piece, or collar; these will need to be taken in or made smaller by the same amount.

Question 124:
Do I need a neckline facing if I have a collar?

Most types of collar require either a partial or full facing around the neckline. They are always sewn to the neckline after the collar has been attached.

A basic shirt collar requires a partial facing that extends from the centre front to the shoulder seams. The back of the neckline doesn't need a facing since it is tucked into the collar and covered with the seam allowance of the collar. A shirt collar with a band does not need a facing either, because the band covers the raw edge of the neckline.

A collar that lies flat against the neckline, such as a Peter Pan collar, works best with a facing around the entire neckline. A mandarin (or stand-up) collar can be sewn without a facing, but adding one may be a better option since it adds extra support around the neckline.

Deciding whether or not to have a facing with a collar will depend on fabric type as well as collar style. If you would like to add a facing and one is not included in your pattern, see Question 127 for how to make a pattern for your own facing.

Question 125:
What does 'stitch-in-the-ditch' mean?

Stitch-in-the-ditch is a technique often used in machine quilting, but which has useful applications in dressmaking as well. The 'ditch' refers to the indentation on the outside of a garment caused by the seam. If you sew along the seam accurately the stitching will be hidden in the 'ditch'.

Stitching in the ditch can be used to sew down a neckline facing; you can stitch in the ditch at the shoulder seam. You can also sew down a waistline facing by stitching in the side seam. In both these cases, you only need to sew a few stitches at the outer edge of the facing. It's also possible to sew down the inner layer of a waistband by stitching in the waistline seam 'ditch' around the entire waist.

To stitch in the ditch, first press the seam allowances either open or to one side. Then put the garment in the sewing machine with right side uppermost; you may need to use pins to hold the seam allowances either open or to one side. As you stitch, keep your eye on the needle so it does not stray to either side of the ditch.

Part of this seam has been 'stitched in the ditch'. If a matching thread had been used (a contrasting colour was used here for clarity) then the stitches would be virtually invisible.

Question 126:
How do I sew a square neckline?

A square neckline should look precise and symmetrical after you've attached a facing or a lining. Start by stay stitching around the raw edges of the garment neckline and facing pieces, and interface the facing. You then need to mark the corners of the square neckline. Lay the garment piece out flat, wrong side up, and use a seam gauge to mark the vertical and horizontal seam allowances; where the marked lines intersect, make a dot – this is the exact corner. Repeat on the facing piece. Then sew the shoulder seams of first the garment pieces and then the facing pieces. Pin the facing to the garment right sides together. Stick a pin through the dots on the garment side to make sure the dots on the facing side match up.

Begin stitching at the centre front or back, depending on where the neck opens. If the opening is in the back, start at the centre front and stitch to one end. Turn the garment over and repeat for the other side. This way, the garment won't hide the seam guides on the throat plate of your sewing machine. Do not begin stitching at the corners. When you reach the corner, stop with your needle in the down position, piercing the marked dot as close to its centre as possible. Raise your presser foot and turn the garment until the seam is realigned with the seam guides on the throat plate; continue to sew. Repeat for the other side.

When you have sewn the entire neckline, check your accuracy by folding the garment in half, so the corners and edges are aligned. Re-stitch if needed. To turn the facing to the inside, clip into the corner from raw edge to the stitching line. Trim and grade (see Question 83) then turn the facing to the right side and press.

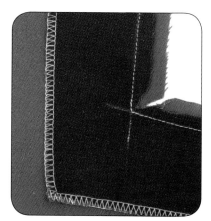

ABOVE After stitching, you need to grade seams and clip into the corners.

Question 127:
If I change the shape of the neckline, how do I make a facing piece to match?

Whenever you change the shape of a neckline, you also have to change the corresponding facing piece to match the new shape. This is an easy process because you can use the adjusted garment pattern piece as a guide.

Start by laying out the pattern piece with the altered neckline. Place a piece of tissue paper on top of the pattern and pin it to the pattern in a few places. Trace around the neck edge and along the shoulder of the pattern. Trace along the centre front and side seams for about 10cm (4in): there is no need to trace round the whole bodice section, you just need the area where the neckline is. Then draw in a line that follows the neckline edge about 7.5cm (3in) in; start the line

at the shoulder and end it at the centre front line. The area between the neckline edge and this new line forms the facing pattern. Add any markings from the original pattern and draw in a grain line to match the one on the pattern piece. Cut out the new facing pattern and use it to cut out your fabric facing.

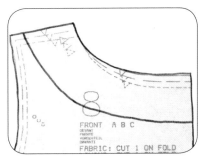

ABOVE Trace your pattern and then draw in the edge of the facing.

EXPERT TIP

66 If you have access to a photocopier, you can make a copy of the altered pattern piece and then draw the new facing directly on to the photocopy. All you need to do then is cut the piece out; any markings will already be on the photocopy. The exception to this may be the grain line; draw this in if it's cut off your photocopy. 99

Question 128:
Can I skip the facing and just turn under the fabric edge?

It is possible to omit a facing, but good results depend very much on the type of fabric you are using and the shape of the edge. Although a straight edge is easy to turn under, omitting the facing may not be a good idea because you will lose the support it provides.

On curved edges, such as at a neckline, knit fabrics can be turned under more easily than woven fabrics. To turn the edge, stay stitch along the seam allowance line and press the edge toward the inside. Trim the seam allowance to 1cm (⅜in); if it doesn't lay flat, clip the curve and apply a fusible web strip between the layers to hold it in place. This may not work well on a woven fabric, because a certain amount of stretch or give is needed to turn the fabric to the inside.

You can also make a bias trim to sew around a neck edge. First cut a bias strip 5cm (2in) wide and as long as the neckline edge. Trim the seam allowance of the neckline to 12mm (½in). Place the bias strip along the neckline edge, right sides together. Stitch the strip to the neckline at 12mm (½in). Press the seam allowance away from the garment and then wrap the bias trim around the seam allowance to the inside. Fold the raw edge under and press. Manipulate the folds as you press to make the width even all around. Stitch down the folded edge of the bias trim on the inside.

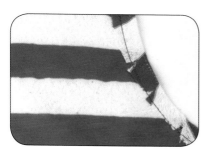

ABOVE You may have to clip into the edge of a knit fabric to make it lie flat.

ABOVE Finish a neckline with a bias trim before turning under and hemming.

Question 129:
What is a bias facing?

A bias facing is a strip of fabric cut on the bias grain and stitched to a raw edge of the garment. The stitch steps are the same as for attaching a shaped facing (see Question 120) except that the strip must be manipulated to fit the shape of the raw edge as you pin it down. To help it fit, clip the seam allowance of the garment edge before you pin and sew the facing down. Sew with the garment side up so you can straighten the clipped edge to fit the bias edge as you sew.

A bias facing is a good option if you want to avoid the bulk that might result at the seam allowance when you add a facing piece. It's also a useful solution if you run out of fabric for facings. You can use a different fabric for a bias facing, such as a lining fabric, but it's a good idea to match the colour to the garment fabric if possible.

To make a bias strip, locate the bias grain on your fabric (see Question 49) and cut a length as long as the facing edge and about 5cm (2in) wide. Sew the strip to the edge, curving it around as needed. Turn to the inside (clipping if needed) and sew down with a topstitch or by hand, trimming the excess width if needed. You don't turn under the bias edge, as in Question 128, and you don't need to finish the outer edge of the facing because the bias will not unravel or fray very much.

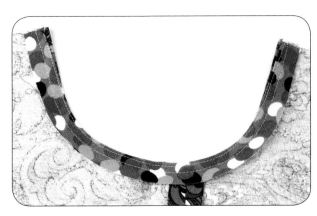

LEFT Once you've stitched the bias facing to the garment, clip the seams and turn it to the inside. Press and then topstitch all round.

Question 130:
How do I prevent a neckline on a stretch fabric from stretching?

It is important to avoid stretching a neckline out of shape while working with it, especially in a knit fabric. Sometimes a stay stitch can cause the fabric to stretch even more rather than hold it in place. This also applies to bias edges on woven fabrics, such as you get with a V-shape neckline.

To avoid this, before you begin to sew the garment together, cut narrow strips of fusible interfacing, 6–12mm (¼–½in) wide, and fuse to the wrong side of the fabric around the neckline edge. Place the strip right over the seam line. Fusible tape on a roll is available for this very purpose. (Cut a swatch on the same grain line and test sew the edge to find the best solution.) The results will vary depending on what type of interfacing or fusible tape you use. Some are straight, others are bias, and still others are made with a knit fabric that has a small amount of give.

After you fuse the tape to the neckline, sew the facing as you normally would. You can also apply the tape to an edge you plan to bind with bias tape, or turn under without a facing.

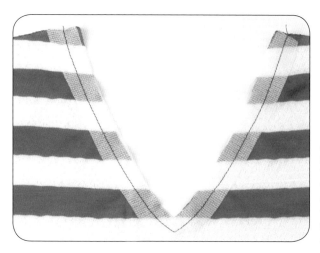

LEFT A strip of suitable interfacing, fused or stitched to the neckline of your garment will help prevent a stretch fabric distorting.

Question 131:
Can I omit or change the shape of the collar?

It is an easy matter to omit the collar from a garment since this does not require any change to the pattern pieces. Instead, you can add a facing, or finish the edge with bias binding, or turn under the neckline edge. It's quite simple to make a facing for the collar if it does not already have one – simply follow the method as outlined in Question 127. You can also add to a partial facing – for example, on an open front shirt that has a facing from the centre front to shoulders, you can add a facing for the back of the neck so you have a facing around the whole neckline.

You can also change the shape of the collar, as long as you do not change the edge that is stitched to the neckline. For example, you can change a collar with points to a collar with rounded edges, simply by redrafting the relevant pattern piece. Make sure the transition from original shape to altered shape is smooth at the edges of the pattern piece; and make sure that the shape is symmetrical.

On a banded shirt collar, you can leave off the larger, outside piece of this two-piece collar and use the band only to make a mandarin collar. Changing collar shapes can create a new look and enhance a tried-and-tested shirt pattern without having to refit.

Question 132:
How do I sew the collar pieces together?

A collar consists of two layers of fabric sewn together, with interfacing fused or stitched to one of the layers. To stitch the collar, first apply the interfacing to one collar piece. Then pin the collar pieces right sides together, matching notches. (One side of a collar is always left unstitched as that will be the side you sew to the neckline edge.)

Stitch around the edges with the interfaced side up. Start at the centre back and stitch toward the corner.

As you get close to the corner, stitch very slowly so you can stop with the needle down, piercing the fabric, exactly in the corner; use the hand wheel if necessary. Raise the presser foot and turn the collar to stitch the rest of the collar edge. Then flip the collar over and stitch the rest of the collar in the same manner, starting at the centre back. Grade the neckline seam and trim the seams at the corners. Turn the collar to the right side and press. Top stitch around the edge if desired.

LEFT When you've stitched the collar pieces together you should trim the seam at the points to make sure you can turn the collar successfully to the right side.

Question 133:
How do I sew a collar with a band?

A collar with a band is usually referred to as a shirt collar, or a collar with a stand. It is most often seen on men's tailored or dress shirts, and on women's shirt-dresses and tailored blouses. The collar consists of a collar sewn to a band that is then attached to the neckline. Both the collar and the band consist of two layers of fabric with interfacing fused or stitched to one of the layers.

To assemble the collar, pin and sew around the outer edges of the collar, leaving the notched edge open (see Question 132). Trim, clip and turn the collar to the outside. Press flat. To join the collar to the band, lay out the interfaced part of the band with the right side of the fabric up, and place the collar on top, with the interfaced side down. Match the notches along

EXPERT TIP

66 **When you sew a banded collar to the neckline, sew just one layer of the band to the neckline – the other layer is turned under at the seam allowance and stitched down later to cover up the neckline seam. When the collar is placed against the neckline, it should be right side up and the under-stitch side down. 99**

the unstitched collar edge. Place the other part of the band right side down on top of the collar, again matching notches along the unstitched collar edge. The collar should be sandwiched between the band pieces. Pin through all the layers, making sure the ends of the band pieces match up. Stitch around the edges, clip curves and turn to the outside; press. The assembled collar is now ready to sew onto the garment neckline.

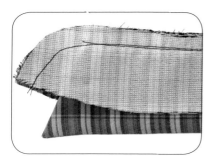

LEFT The collar part of a band collar should be sandwiched between the band sections before stitching.

Question 134:
What is an under collar?

Some patterns will contain two separate pieces for the collar: an under layer and an upper layer. The under layer is called an under collar and it is slightly smaller (by about 2mm ($^1/_{16}$in) around all the edges) than the upper layer. This is so that when the collar is turned to the right side, the layers are properly aligned. The slightly smaller size of the under collar, when stitched to the neckline, pulls the upper collar layer slightly underneath so it doesn't show on the outside.

Under collars are usually found in more tailored garments and only on rolled collars, such as shirt collars, notched lapel collars and shawl collars. Because of the roll of these collars, the upper collar needs to be larger than the under collar, so the edges of the upper roll over the edges of the under when finished.

An under collar is sometimes cut as two pieces, both on the bias, joined together with a centre seam. The bias cut helps the under collar fit more easily and smoothly against the upper collar when they are sewn together.

Question 135:
How do I make nice, sharp points on a collar?

Matching collar points are essential on a shirt if you want to create a professional-looking finish. When a shirt is being worn, the collar ends meet at the centre front and are a particularly noticeable feature of the garment.

After cutting out the collar pieces and before you remove the pins, mark the stitch lines on the pieces so you can see where they intersect at the point. (When you apply the collar interfacing make sure you fuse or stitch it to the unmarked layer so you don't cover up the markings.) If you do require interfacing on both layers, you will have to mark the stitch lines after applying the interfacing.

When you stitch the collar pieces together, shorten the stitch length at about 12mm (½in) before and after you get to points. Clip the points at a sharp angle in each direction, and grade the seams close to the points to remove as much bulk as possible before you turn the collar to the outside. To help turn the points, use a point turner and gently push out the points. Don't use the point of your scissors since you may poke a hole through the fabric. If you still need to sharpen the point once you have turned the collar to the outside, pick the point outwards with a pin, but do this carefully so you don't create a hole in the fabric.

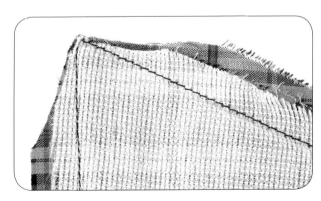

LEFT After stitching, trim the seam at the point at a sharp angle. Grade the seams at the same time to further reduce bulk.

Question 136:
How do I stitch a curved collar?

A curved collar is stitched in the same manner as most collars, except that you must turn the fabric gradually and smoothly as you stitch around the curved seam edge. It can be tricky to stitch the curve so that it looks smooth and balanced on both ends of the collar so you may want to practise stitching a curve before you start (see Question 82). To do this, cut out a circle from a scrap of fabric and place it in the sewing machine. Try stitching around the edge while maintaining a consistent seam allowance (see Tip below).

Once you are happy with the technique, move on to stitching the collar pieces together (see Question 132). Before you begin, you could mark the stitching line on your pieces with chalk and then follow this line as a guide. When the stitching is completed, fold the collar in half to match the curved ends and verify that the two curves are the same shape. If not, go back and re-stitch one or both of the curves so they match. Then clip the seam allowance every 1cm (⅜in), up to but not through the stitch line (see Question 83). Cut wedge shapes into the allowance around the sharpest part of the collar curves to reduce the bulk of the seam. Turn the collar to the right side and push out the curved seam gently with a blunt tip, such as a point turner. Do not use your scissors to do this; the sharp tip might make a hole. Press the collar flat, making sure the seam is pushed out completely.

EXPERT TIP

66 To stitch a smooth curve, keep the curved edge of the fabric aligned with the stitch guide to the right of the needle on the throat plate. Stitch slowly as you turn the fabric with your left hand. For best results, turn the fabric just a bit sooner than you think you need to, still keeping it aligned with the stitch guide line that matches the width of your seam allowance. 99

Question 137:
What is a mandarin collar?

Also known as a stand-up or a band collar, a mandarin collar is a simpler style that can be used in tailored jackets, dresses, or even casual knitted garments. The width of the collar can vary, according to what is most flattering to the body type – if you have a short neck then a narrower mandarin collar will be more suitable. Where the collar meets at the centre front of the neckline the corners can be either curved or at a right angle.

When sewing together the pieces of a mandarin collar it is important to be sure that the ends match one another, since any discrepancy will be instantly noticeable at the centre front neckline of your garment.

A mandarin collar can be made from a traditional, two-piece shirt collar that consists of a neckband as well as the collar piece itself. If you wish to convert a traditional two-piece collar to a mandarin, you simply omit the main collar piece and attach just the band to the neckline. A mandarin collar is a stylish addition to any garment, so consider expanding your dressmaking creativity by including this classic design feature!

ABOVE A mandarin collar is ideal for a military-style jacket or coat that features several other design details.

Question 138:
What is a 'Peter Pan' collar?

Unlike a mandarin or stand-up collar, a 'Peter Pan' collar sits flat against the outside of a neckline. (The name is derived from the costume worn by Peter Pan, the character from children's literature.) Peter Pan collars are usually made from a fabric that's a contrasting colour, such as white, to the jacket, dress or shirt to which they are being attached.

The collar usually has rounded edges meeting at the centre front, but can also have rounded points. Either of these can be sewn to a round or V-neck. The main feature of this type of collar is that it has very little or no stand, unlike a shirt collar that rolls to the outside. It is assembled the same as a shirt collar, but because it is flat, it sits wider against the garment.

LEFT A Peter Pan collar is an ideal finish for pretty, feminine-style blouse. This type of collar is often made in different fabric to the rest of the garment.

Question 139:
How do I sew a collar to the neckline?

The collar edge must be sewn exactly to the neckline, so it is important to sew seam allowances accurately on both the collar and shoulder seams. The first step is to stay stitch (see Question 71) around the raw edge of the neckline and clip the seam allowance (see Question 83) every 12mm (½in). This helps the neckline flatten out so it can be pinned to the collar.

Mark the centre back of the neckline and the centre of the collar raw edge as well. (A quick way to find the centre of the collar is to fold it in half.) Lay the garment right side up on a flat surface with the neck curve pulled flat. Pin the interfaced layer of the collar band to the neckline, right sides together, matching centre backs and notches. (Don't catch the other layer of the band). Start pinning at the centre back and work your way toward each collar end. Don't be afraid to use lots of pins. Whenever you pin a flat edge (collar) to a round edge (neckline) it takes patience and manipulation of fabric on both sides to match them accurately.

Make sure the collar ends match up with the centre fronts of the shirt. To verify, fold the shirt and collar in half, to see if they match up at the centre front. Press seam allowance towards the band, away from the shirt. Fold the seam allowance of the other band under and stitch down across the length of the neckline. Since this stitching will show on the outside of the collar band, pin this section carefully before you sew.

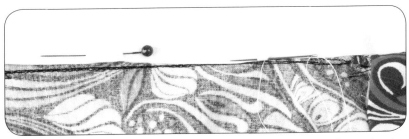

ABOVE When you sew the edge of the collar to the neckline, take small, even hand stitches along both edges.

Question 140:
How do I sew an unlined patch pocket?

A patch pocket is cut into a desired shape and all raw edges are finished before stitching to the garment. To sew a plain shirt pocket, turn under and press the upper edge by 6mm (¼in); stitch. Fold over the same edge to the outside by 2cm (¾in). Stitch down the fold on each side, taking a 6mm (½in) seam allowance (see bottom left). Clip corners and trim the seam allowance. Turn the fold to the right side. To sharpen the corners, carefully 'pick' the points out with a pin.

If you wish, topstitch across the pocket on the outside to hold the fold down. Turn and press under the remaining edges of the pocket by 6mm (½in). The pocket has now been finished on all sides. Pin it on the garment where desired

EXPERT TIP

❝ To make pockets that match exactly, work on the ironing board with pins and seam gauge to hand. As you fold and press, keep the pockets lined up next to each other so you can keep them aligned. ❞

and stitch down, starting from one upper corner (see bottom right). At each lower corner, stop with your needle down, raise the presser foot, pivot the pocket until the foot is lined up with the next edge, lower your presser foot, and continue stitching. (See Question 126 for how to turn corners or stitch a square).

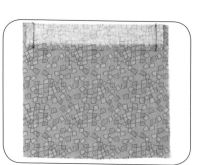

ABOVE Hem the top edge of the pocket and then turn down, to the right side.

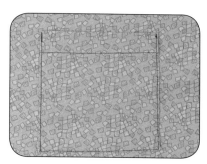

ABOVE After turning the top to the right side, stitch the pocket in place.

Question 141:
How do I sew a lined patch pocket?

A lined patch pocket is a good option if you are using a loosely woven fabric or one that unravels easily. The lining creates a clean finish that is precise around all the edges and are therefore ideal for unique or novelty shaped pockets.

For the lining, choose one in a colour that closely matches the garment fabric. Cut one shape in fabric and one in lining for each pocket. Pin and stitch right sides together, leaving an opening of 5cm (2in) or less on one edge: if the shape is not a square, leave the opening on the bottom edge

where it is less conspicuous. Trim the seams and clip corners and curves. Turn the pocket to the right side through the opening and press, making sure the lining is not visible from the right side.

You don't have to sew the opening closed, because it will be secured when you sew the pocket to the garment. (The hand stitching you would use to do this has to be very accurate not to show on the outside.) Position the pocket on the garment front with pins and stitch around three sides, leaving it open at the top.

LEFT Stitch the lining to the fabric pocket piece, leaving a gap in one side for turning to the right side. Snip across the corners and trim seams.

Question 142:
How do I sew a patch pocket with a flap?

You can add a flap to a patch pocket easily, using the size of the finished pocket as a guide. To work out the right size of the pieces, measure the finished opening of the pocket and add 6mm (½in) for overlap on each side (3mm (¼in) times two). For thicker fabrics, add 2.5cm (1in). Then add 12mm (½in) around all edges for seam allowance. Cut two flap pieces in fabric, or one in fabric and one in lining if the fabric is thick.

Put both flap pieces right sides together and stitch around three sides at 12mm (½in); trim, clip and turn right side out. Attach the patch pocket to the garment first (see Question 140), then centre the raw edge of the flap, right side down, just above the pocket opening – it should extend slightly past each side of the pocket. Stitch the flap down across the raw edge at 12mm (½in). Trim out the corners of the seam allowance and then press the flap down over the pocket opening. Topstitch across the flap, 12mm (½in) from the fold to keep the flap down – make sure you don't stitch across the top of the actual pocket.

ABOVE Once you've made a flap, centre it above the pocket, right side down, and stitch in place.

Question 143:
How do I sew a patch pocket with rounded edges?

A rounded patch pocket is prepared and stitched in the same manner as an unlined square pocket, (see Question 140) but to make the rounded edges symmetrical requires an extra step, especially if you are making more than one pocket and you want them to match perfectly.

After you have finished the upper edge of the pocket opening (see Question 140) but before you turn the remaining edges under, machine tack around the curved edges. Pull slightly on the threads to draw up the curved edges and then press them to the inside at 12mm (½in).

If you are making two or more pockets, line them up on your pressing surface to make sure they match. Press flat; turn over to the right side. If you are making more than one pocket, lay one over the other to verify their symmetry. Position the pocket(s) on the garment where desired. Pin and stitch down.

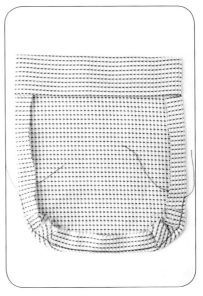

ABOVE After finishing the top edge of the pocket, machine tack the curved edges and use the tacking to draw up the fabric at the corners.

Question 144:
How do I add a pocket in a side seam?

A side seam pocket has two identical pieces that are hidden once they are sewn into a seam. If your pattern does not include a pocket, the pieces are easy to cut and add to the garment. To reduce bulk, cut the pocket from a lining fabric. Before you begin, reinforce the pocket opening at the side seam with fusible or sew-in stay tape.

If you are adding this pocket, the pattern will not have placement markings, so be sure to position the opening accurately for comfortable hand placement.

Stitch one pocket piece, right sides together to the back garment piece at the side seam. Repeat with the front garment piece. Under stitch the front pocket only. Press the seam allowances and the pieces outward. Place the garment front on the garment back, rights sides together, lining up the side seams and pocket edges. Stitch the side seams and around the pocket edges. Clip into the back seam at the upper and lower corners. Press the side seam open and the pocket toward the front.

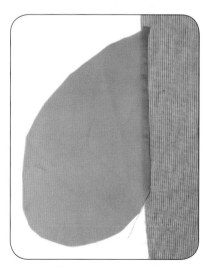

ABOVE After stitching the pocket piece to the back, press it outwards.

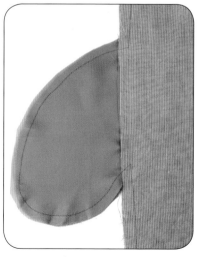

ABOVE Put the back and front pieces together and stitch the seams.

Question 145:
How do I sew a side front pocket?

A side front pocket is the type found in casual skirts or jeans. The opening is slanted or curved. The facing for the opening can be cut from lining fabric and the side front piece (sometimes called a yoke) is cut from the garment fabric since it shows on the outside.

Reinforce the pocket front edge with a strip of fusible interfacing to prevent stretching. Pin the facing to the pocket edge only, right sides together – not to the side or waist (upper edge). Under stitch on the facing side; then turn the facing to the inside. Press and topstitch along the edge if desired.

Lay the front of the garment flat, with the pocket facing opened out. Place the yoke piece on top of the pocket piece, matching the side and waist edges. Pin and stitch around the curved edges of the pocket pieces only – do not sew the pocket to the garment itself. Turn the pocket back under the front section and stitch down at the waist edge. Now you are ready to sew the garment front to the garment back at the side seams.

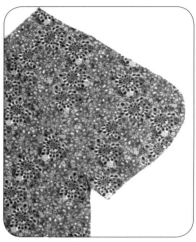

ABOVE When the pocket facing is stitched to the front, open it out.

ABOVE Place the pocket yoke on the pocket facing and stitch round the edge.

Question 146:
How do I add a welt pocket?

First cut out three pieces of fabric – for the purposes of this illustration each piece is 7.5 x 18cm (3 x 7in). Cut one piece of interfacing 7.5 x 18cm (3 x 7in) and one piece of lining 28 x 18cm (11 x 7in). Fuse the interfacing on the wrong side of the garment at the pocket placement. Mark the pocket placement on the interfacing with chalk. Machine tack over the markings so you have an elongated 'H' shape (step 1). The cross-bar of the H is the desired width of the pocket opening – in this case it's 12.5cm (5in).

Turn the garment over to its right side. Take one fabric strip and centre it on the pocket marking, so one edge of the fabric lines up with the H cross-bar. Stitch 1cm (⅜in) from the H cross-bar, starting and stopping exactly on the uprights of the H – the stitched line should be exactly 12.5cm (5in) long. Place another fabric strip on the opposite side of the pocket marking, so it butts up to strip just stitched down. Stitch in place as before. Machine tack across both fabric strips, 1cm (⅜in) from the first stitched lines (step 2).

Fold each fabric strip towards the pocket marking and press flat. Stitch 1cm (⅜in) in from the fold, sewing right over the stitch line in step 2. (If you stitch from the wrong side, you will be able to stitch exactly over the line.) Start and stop exactly on the uprights of the H (step 3).

Cut along the cross-bar of the H shape, through the garment fabric only, keeping the pocket strips (the welts) out of the way (step 4). Stop 2.5cm (1in) from each end then cut diagonal lines out towards the ends of the H uprights to form triangles of fabric at each end of the slit. Remove any tacking stitches.

Turn the welts to the wrong side of the garment through the slit. Press so the welts lie flat on the wrong side. Tuck the triangle shapes at the end of each slit under the welts. Stitch round the welts, close to the opening, to secure them to the turnings – but do not stitch them to the garment (step 5).

Take the remaining fabric strip and place it on the lining piece, right side up and with the top edge of the fabric 2.5cm (1in) below the upper edge of the lining. Stitch all round the sides of the fabric, 12mm (½in) in from the edge (step 6). Place the garment wrong side up and pin the upper edge of the lining piece to the seam allowance of the upper welt; stitch. Stitch the bottom edge of the lining piece to the seam allowance of the lower welt. Press the now-folded lining piece and stitch along the sides (step 7).

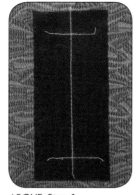

ABOVE Step 1.

ABOVE Step 2.

ABOVE Step 3.

ABOVE Step 4.

ABOVE Step 5.

ABOVE Step 6.

ABOVE Step 7.

8
TUCKS, PLEATS
AND GATHERS

Question 147:
What is the difference between a pleat and a tuck?

Pleats and tucks are folds of fabric that are stitched down to control fullness in a garment as well as add interest and texture.

Tucks can very in width and are stitched down, parallel to the fold, all or part of the way. The stitched folds create texture and add decoration while controlling fullness and shaping the garment to the body. Tucks are best sewn on the lengthwise or crosswise grain. Tucks which are sewn on the bias will stretch out of shape.

Pleats are also folded in various widths, but are stitched down across the top of the folds to hold them in place. The fullness of the fabric is taken in by the folds but also expands to fit the body. Pleats can be pressed the entire length of the fold, or left unpressed to create a softer look in the garment. If you find that your fabric does not press well or hold the pleat shape as much as you would like, edge stitch along the pleat folds for a clean, crisp look.

Question 148:
What types of tucks can I sew?

Various types of tucks include pin tucks, blind tucks, dart tucks (or release tucks), cross tucks and shell tucks. All of them begin with a fold of fabric that is stitched down all or part of the way.

The most common tuck is a pin tuck, which is narrow and sewn on the lengthwise or crosswise grain, several in a row, and evenly spaced

ABOVE After folding and pressing, pin tucks are stitched parallel to the fold.

apart. Blind tucks are stitched so that each tuck overlaps the next.

Dart tucks, also known as release tucks, are stitched in place of a dart, but are left unstitched at the point. The open end of a dart tuck creates the fullness needed to accommodate the shaped area. For example, instead of sewing a bust dart all the way to the point, stop 2.5cm (1in) from the point to 'release' or open up the tuck. For added interest, you can divide the bust dart into two smaller release tucks, though if you do this, make sure the two widths equal the width of the original dart.

ABOVE When blind tucks are stitched down the folds overlap.

ABOVE Dart tucks are used instead of darts and left unstitched at the point.

Question 149:
How do I make pin tucks?

When adding tucks to a garment, stitch the tucks to a width of fabric before cutting out the pattern piece. First, decide on the size of the tucks and the spacing between each one. Make sure the width of the fabric is enough to accommodate the pattern piece after sewing the tucks. Mark the location of each fold along the top edge of the fabric piece, then replicate the markings that are on the top edge on the bottom edge.

Fold the fabric lengthwise at the markings; press the folds in place and then stitch. Press the folds again, in the desired direction – if at the centre front, press half to the left and half to the right – and stay stitch across the top and bottom.

To cut out the pattern, lay it over the tucks and centre them where desired. If the pattern piece has a fold, be sure to fold the fabric as well before cutting. Continue to follow the assembly instructions.

Question 150:
What kinds of pleats can I sew?

Pleats, like tucks, have several varieties, including knife pleats, accordion pleats, box pleats and inverted pleats.

Knife pleats are the most common type of pleat and are also known as side pleats. They are evenly spaced and the folds lay in one direction. They are commonly placed on a skirt at the waist and can be partially stitched down.

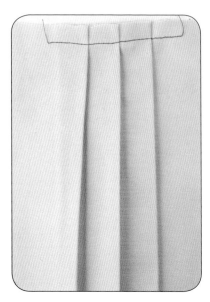

ABOVE Knife pleats are the same size and evenly spaced.

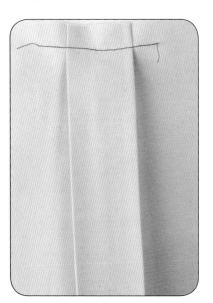

ABOVE The folds of a box pleat face in opposite directions.

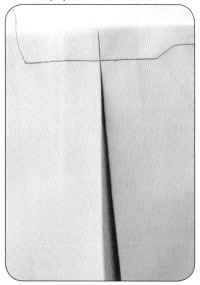

ABOVE The folds of an inverted pleat face in towards each other.

Accordion pleats lie in one direction and are pressed rather than left soft; they should be sharp, crisp and close together, resembling the bellows of an accordion.

Box pleats are formed by two folds in the fabric, facing in opposite directions from each other. Inverted pleats are formed by two folds turned toward each other to meet in the centre. The process of creating these two pleat types is the same – the difference is whether you fold them with the fabric right side up or right side down. A box pleat turned over is an inverted pleat.

Question 151:
How do I get pleats just right?

The most important aspect of creating beautiful pleats begins at the marking stage. (Unlike tucks, the stitching that holds the folds down is done across the upper edge, within the seam allowance.) Pattern pieces that include pleats will be marked with fold lines, stitch lines and arrows pointing in the direction which the pleats should be folded. When you transfer these marks to your fabric pieces, be sure to distinguish between the three. For instance, use solid lines and broken lines, or even different colours of chalk. Use a thin but visible marking tool – a sharp pencil or sharp corner of tailor's chalk is ideal.

Working on a flat surface, pin each fold separately with the pins parallel to the fold. If you are going to partially sew the pleats flat to the garment, do so after you sew across the upper edge. Finally if you are not stitching the folds, except at the top to hold them in place, you can press them crisp, or leave them free for a softer look.

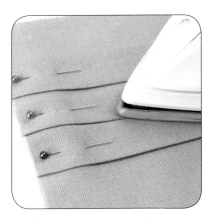

ABOVE Pressing pleats flat after folding will give a crisp finish.

Question 152:
How do I stitch gathers?

Gathers add a soft fullness to portions of a garment by drawing up a fabric edge before sewing it into a smaller edge. The gathers are created by pulling on rows of tacking stitches sewn in the seam allowance. Gathers can be stitched into a waistline on a skirt, cuffs on a full-length sleeve, a back yoke, or any garment area that can accommodate fullness.

To create the gathers, machine tack along the seam line and again 6mm (¼in) away from the seam line. Do not backstitch, but leave a thread tail at both ends of the stitch lines. Draw up the fabric by pulling on the bobbin threads of the two stitch lines. As you pull, move the fabric along the seam line, so the gathers are distributed evenly.

Alternatively, run a line of hand tacking stitches along the seam line, securing the thread well at the end. Then pull on the free end of the thread to gather up the fabric.

Match notches and cross seams when you pin the gathered edge to the smaller edge. Once you have the gathers pinned in place, press lightly in the seam allowance only to flatten them just a bit – this makes it easier to sew them down. After sewing the gathered seam, you may want to reduce the bulk by finishing the seam with a zigzag stitch, overlock stitch, or binding it with bias tape.

ABOVE Stitch two rows of machine tacking and then draw up the stitches to gather the fabric.

ABOVE Alternatively, work a row of hand tacking stitches and then pull on the loose end to gather the fabric.

Question 153:
Can I change a dart to a gather?

A dart can be changed to small gathers without compromising the fit and shaping that the dart is designed to do. This is a good option if you want to avoid the sharp line of a dart, or just want to create a softer look. It's ideal, for example, if you try it on a side bust dart when the fabric is flimsy or stretchy; the gathers disappear into the shaped area when the garment is worn. It also works well when used as a substitute for a bust dart in an empire waistline, or even if you want to convert pleats to gathers on a cuff.

Start by marking the position of the dart with tailor's chalk. Then work a row of machine tacking across the base of the dart, within the seam allowance; start and end the stitching about 2.5cm (1in) on either side of the dart lines. Pin the two edges together before you gather the threads. Draw up the tacking to fit the dart edge to the other edge as you pin the gathers down. Then stitch the seam as you normally would. This method also works well for sheers and other delicate fabrics in which it can be tricky to sew dart points.

ABOVE Use machine tacking to gather up the fullness of the dart when you pin the seam in place. Then machine stitch as normal, over the gathers.

Question 154:
How do I measure and cut a ruffle?

A ruffle is a straight piece of fabric that is finished on either side, gathered up and stitched to the garment for a decorative effect. To determine the size of the ruffle piece, measure the edge to which it will be sewn and double or triple that amount, depending on the fullness you desire. The thinner the garment fabric, the more length you need. The cut width is also whatever you choose, with 2.5cm (1in) added for a hem on either edge.

If you are not sure about how much length to cut, or the fullness you want, experiment with a test piece 30cm (12in) long and 7.5–10cm (3–4in) wide. Machine tack along the length and gather it up to the desired fullness. Measure the gathered length and compare to the original length (30cm (12in)). Then apply the same ratio to cut your ruffle: if, for example, the ungathered edge of 30cm (12in) becomes 10cm (4in) when gathered, it means you will need three times the length to achieve a similar fullness in your ruffle.

Cut ruffles on the lengthwise or crosswise grain and use a rotary cutter for accurate edges. You can try a ruffle cut on bias grain but it may not hold the gathers well.

LEFT A ruffle, when used as a trim, adds a softness to the line of a garment, as well as a decorative touch.

Question 155:
How do I add a ruffle to the edge of a neckline or hem?

Adding a ruffle to a neckline or hem is easy to do, even if your pattern does not include one. To add a ruffle, first measure and cut the desired amount as described in Question 154.

For a neckline, turn under and stitch a narrow hem on one long edge and on each short end of the ruffle. Fold the ruffle in half width ways and mark the centre point. On one long edge, machine two rows of tacking stitches and gather the edge (see Question 152) and pin to the raw edge of the neckline, wrong side of ruffle to right side of garment.

Move the gathers evenly, matching centre points and ends to the neckline; pin and stitch. Then sew the facing to the neckline according to the pattern guidelines.

When adding a ruffle to a hem, bear in mind how the ruffle will look in proportion to the garment length. A full or long skirt may require a wider ruffle than a narrow skirt or short skirt. Hem both long edges of the ruffle and join the short ends to make a loop. Machine tack along the centre, to gather up the fullness before pinning and stitching round the hem.

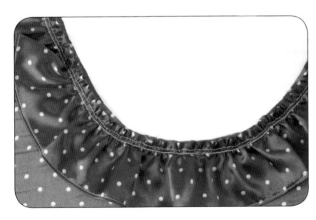

LEFT On a neckline, gather up your ruffle and then stitch to the right side of the garment before finishing the neck edge with a facing.

Question 156:
What is a flounce?

A flounce, like a ruffle, is a separate piece of fabric that adds fullness when sewn to the garment. The volume, however, is created by how it is cut rather than by gathering up fabric with rows of stitches. While a ruffle piece is straight, a flounce is cut as a circle or semi-circle. It has an inner edge and an outer edge: the inner edge is sewn to a straight edge, such as a hem or neckline, and the outer edge is hemmed.

The circumference of the inner circle should be the same measurement as the edge to which it is sewn. A small inner circle gives you less length than a big inner circle. For a very full look, several circles can be stitched together end to end before attaching to the garment You can cut out as many circles as you need to achieve the desired length.

A sheer or drapey fabric can accommodate greater fullness (and more circles stitched together) than a more weighty fabric. The bigger the inner circle, the softer the volume of the flounce.

EXPERT TIP

66 **For maximum fullness, add rows of gathering stitches to the inner circle after you have pieced them together. A flounce like this is also called a circular ruffle. 99**

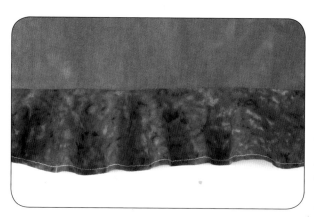

LEFT The top edge of a flounce is the same length as the garment edge to which it's sewn. All the fullness in the flounce comes from the greater length of its outer edge.

Question 157:
How do I cut and sew a flounce?

Determine the size flounce you want by first measuring the edge to which it will be sewn. This is your inner circle measurement. Then decide on the width of the flounce and this amount is the distance of the inner circle to the outer circle. Using a large sheet of tissue paper, draw the inner circle first and add the seam allowance inside the circle. Draw the outer circle and add the seam allowance outside the circle. Then draw a straight line from the inner circle to the outer circle. Cut out the shape to make your flounce pattern.

On your fabric, place the straight line you drew on your pattern on the lengthwise grain and pin it in place. Pin around the rest of the pattern. Cut around the outer circle first and then cut the inner circle.

Hem the outer edge. Stay stitch around the inner circle and clip the seam allowance until the inner edge can be pulled out straight. Pin and sew to the garment edge.

EXPERT TIP

66 If you don't have a compass to draw a perfect circle, use a round object with a circumference that matches the inner circle measurement. Or, tie a string around the tip of a pencil, hold the other end of the string with your finger in the centre of the circle, and then move the pencil around to draw the circle. 99

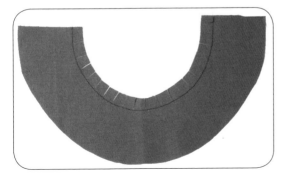

LEFT After cutting out your flounce, stay stitch around the inner edge and clip into the curve to make it easier to fit the flounce to a straight edge.

9
WAISTBANDS

Question 158:
How do I sew a straight waistband?

A straight waistband is simple to cut and sew. The fabric can be cut out as a single piece or cut as two pieces joined at a centre back seam. For the greatest stability, cut it on the lengthwise grain.

Before you attach a waistband to the top of your skirt, first stitch together all the skirt pieces. Then press flat the darts and seams at the waistline. Stay stitch around the edge of the waistband, right along the stitch line. Apply stabiliser (see Question 159) to the wrong side of the band.

Pin and sew the band to the waistline of the skirt, matching notches and markings. It is easier to start at the centre back and work outwards to either end. You do not have to clip the waistline seam allowance, unless you are sewing a full, circular skirt.

Try on the garment to check the fit of the band. If you're happy, finish off the ends of the waistband. Fold the waistband in half lengthwise, right sides together and stitch across the short ends. If you are using a monofilament interfacing, do not include it in the stitching; rather, cut it off just inside the seam line. Clip the top-most corners, to reduce bulk and turn the waistband to the outside; press.

On the inside of the garment, turn under the seam allowance on the raw edge of the waistband and pin in place. Hand sew or machine stitch the fold in place. If hand stitching, you can make your stitches in the seam allowance at the top of the skirt, so they won't be visible on the right side.

Question 159:
What type of stabiliser should I use in the waistband?

The most common way to stabilise a waistband is with fusible interfacing. Choose one that matches the weight of the fabric. Most straight waistbands are folded lengthwise in the middle, but the interfacing should cover the entire width, so you have two layers of interfacing on the inside when the band is completed.

Another option is non-fusible, polyester monofilament instead of interfacing. It is stiffer than interfacing, but does not create extra bulk or discomfort when worn. Monofilament can be purchased by the length and is most commonly 2.5cm (1in) wide. This is a good width for straight waistbands but it can be trimmed down if desired.

To sew the monofilament to the waistband, place one long edge along the lengthwise centre fold. Stitch close to the edge. (The stitching will show on the outside of the band). Stitch close to the other edge near the seam allowance. The width of the stabiliser extends only to the fold, or one half the width of the band piece. (So when the waistband is done, the stabiliser is one layer, rather than two.)

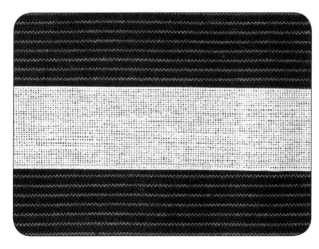

LEFT Stitch both lengthwise edges of a non-fusible stabiliser onto your waistband strip. The top edge stitching will be visible on the right side. The bottom edge will sit in the seam allowance.

Question 160:
How do I make a waistline stay?

A waistline stay does just what its name says – it holds the waist of a dress in place so it doesn't slip or drop while being worn. It also relieves stress on a dress closure, such as the zip. It is especially useful on strapless dresses as it helps prevent the wearer having to tug on the top of the dress to keep it up.

To make the stay, cut a strip of grosgrain ribbon the length of the waist measurement plus 5cm (2in) for overlap at each end. Sew a sturdy hook and eye at either end (like the ones used on a skirt or trouser waistband). On the inside of the garment, stitch the corresponding hook and eye parts at the waistline closure. Then secure the ends of the waistline stay inside the dress to this hook and eye before wearing it. For greater security, stitch the ribbon to the side seams at the waist.

ABOVE The hook and eye on a waistline stay are attached to a corresponding eye and hook at the waist's closure. Stitching down the stay at the seams adds security.

Question 161:
I have attached the waistband but it is too big; what do I do?

You can end up with a waistband that's too big if you did not check its length before sewing it to the skirt or dress. To make the waistband fit, first remove it from the garment and wrap it around the waist (or the upper hip for a contoured waistband) so it is comfortably snug but not tight. Pin the ends together at the closure to form a seam allowance that faces outward. Chalk mark where the pins are as well as the position of the seams in relation to the waistband. Remove the waistband and turn it to the wrong side. Pin to the garment, matching chalk marks.

If the garment is too big to fit the waistband, you can take it in a little at the side seams and maybe at the darts (only a little though; take in too much at the darts and you could spoil the fit). You could also ease it into the waistband; run tacking stitches around the stitch line of the garment waistline and pull on the end of the thread to gently gather up the fabric until it fits inside the waistband.

Re-stitch the waistband to the skirt. Stitch across the short ends again, clipping across the corners. Turn the waistband to the inside of the skirt and stitch in place. Instead of fitting the waistband to the garment, you are fitting the garment to the waistband after it has been accurately fitted and marked.

Question 162:
Can I eliminate the waistband?

If your pattern has a waistband you can leave it off, but the waistline must be finished in another way. Adding a facing eliminates the need for a waistband but still gives support at the waist. After stitching together the skirt front pieces (if necessary) and stitching in any darts, place the skirt front wrong side up and put tissue paper on top. Trace around the top of the waistline and then down the sides for about 10cm (4in). Draw a line 10cm (4in) below the waistline. This creates the front facing pattern; repeat with the back of the skirt to make a pattern for the back facing. Use the patterns to cut out two pieces of fabric. Be sure to match the grain line on the facing pieces with the grain line on the

skirt. And remember to add seam allowances at the short ends.

Alternatively, stitch a bias facing (see Question 169) to the waistline. Clip the seam, understitch and turn to the inside; secure at the cross seams. No matter what option you choose, add a stabiliser to the waist seam, such as stay tape, since this area tends to stretch during wear.

EXPERT TIP

❝ If you want a faced waist but have run out of fabric, you could make a facing from another fabric that is similar in weight (and colour, if possible). ❞

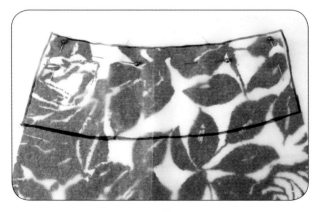

LEFT Make a pattern for a skirt waist facing by tracing over the top edge of your completed skirt front and back.

Question 163:
Can I add a waistband if one isn't included in the pattern?

A straight waistband is the simplest type of waistband to add, but you can also create a contoured waistband by drafting your own pattern, just as you would a waistline facing on a skirt.

To make a straight waistband, first measure the length of the waistline on the skirt pattern (not your own waistline). Add on 7.5cm (3in) for seam allowances and an overlap at the closure. Decide on how deep you would like the waistband and then multiply this amount by two; add on 2.5cm (1in) for seam allowances.

Use these dimensions to draw out a long rectangle shape on a large piece of tissue paper. Make sure the long edges of your rectangle run parallel to each other, maintaining a consistent width along the whole length of the waistband. Mark the lengthwise centre line so you know where to fold the fabric after cutting out. You can also use this line to position the pattern piece on the fabric grain. Cut out your pattern and use it to cut out one piece of fabric for the waistband. Stabilise and stitch in place as described in Questions 158 and 159.

To add a band to a curved or contoured waistline, follow the steps for making a waistline facing to create the pattern for the band. Cut two sets of pieces, plus one set for interfacing. To assemble the band and sew to the garment, follow the steps outlined in Questions 167 and 168.

Knowing how to make your own waistband expands your options on many styles that may be just right, except for a missing waistband.

Question 164:
How do I sew an elastic waistband?

An elastic waistband is designed primarily for comfort and so it should be sewn and fitted with that in mind. It requires a casing into which the elastic is placed after the casing is stitched to the garment. The casing can be an extension of the waistline or added as a separate piece. Before you sew, decide on the width (unless the pattern has determined this for you) of the finished waistband, which is also the elastic width. The extension of fabric required for the casing is two times this, plus 2cm (¾in).

Put on the skirt or dress and wrap a generous length of the elastic around the waist, over the fabric. Pin elastic in place for a comfortable fit. Chalk mark the waist at the lower edge of the elastic. Mark the length

> ## EXPERT TIP
> 66 **To prevent the elastic from slipping or rolling, stitch in the ditch (see Question 125) through all the layers at the vertical seams.** 99

of the elastic as well, but with 5cm (2in) for overlap.

Remove the garment and lie it out flat. Measure and mark the casing width above the chalk mark. Cut off the excess. (If there isn't enough fabric, sew on a separate casing piece with extra width for seam allowances.)

Turn the upper edge under 12mm (½in) and press. Fold again to the inside so the folded edge meets the waistline chalk marks. This forms the casing. Pin and stitch close to the fold, leaving a 5cm (2in) opening in the back of the waistband. Use a bodkin to thread the elastic through the casing. Pin the elastic ends together and try on again. Adjust if needed. Sew the elastic ends with a 2.5cm (1in) overlap. Tuck the elastic back in to the casing and stitch the opening closed.

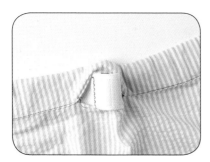

ABOVE Overlap the ends of the elastic and stitch together.

Question 165:
What type of elastic should I buy?

Elastic comes in a variety of widths, types and weights. It should be chosen according to the type of fabric and where it is utilised on the garment. Some of the most common types include braided, knit and clear elastics.

Braided elastic is durable and does not roll up easily, but it can be weakened when stitched down if the sewing-machine needle you use breaks the strands. To avoid this, use a ballpoint needle when sewing braided elastic.

Knit elastic is softer and therefore more comfortable for knits and lighter weight fabrics. It may curl but it is less likely to break when stitched through. Clear elastic is very stretchy and useful for sewing on seams that require give and memory to return to their original length after stretch during wear. It works well on shoulder seams, in seams on knits and on bathing suits.

EXPERT TIP

❝ To sew bathing suits, use cotton braided elastic, which is designed to hold up better when exposed to chlorine and sunlight. ❞

LEFT Elastic comes in a wide variety of widths and types, suitable for a wide range of different purposes and garments.

Question 166:
How do I measure the amount of elastic I need?

Since elastic types vary in stretch and recovery, it is always a good idea to check the length of elastic you need before stitching permanently in place. Even if you have measured the circumference of the area where it is to be worn, and marked it properly, chances are the fit will change a bit after the elastic is attached to the fabric.

Also, you need to verify that the elastic (and the garment) will stretch enough for you to put it on and take it off comfortably. For instance, can you remove the skirt after the elastic is inserted? Or, on a short sleeve hem, does it pinch the arm? When sewing elastic to a wrist, wrap the elastic around your fist to make sure it will stretch enough to slip over your hand.

EXPERT TIP

66 Avoid sewing the elastic through the casing until you have double-checked the fit. It is difficult to remove stitches in elastic once it has been sewn down. To secure the elastic without sewing multiple rows, stitch in the ditch at the cross seams. 99

Question 167:
How do I sew a curved waistband?

A curved or contoured waistband differs from a straight or elastic waistband because it contains several pieces that are stitched together and shaped to match the curve of the hip. The waistband consists of two sets of pieces, one each for an upper and under band. The upper band is interfaced. The under band can also be interfaced if the fabric looks or feels like it needs more stabiliser.

Join the upper band pieces at the side and back seams, matching notches. Repeat for the under band pieces. Wrap the upper band around the hip area to verify a snug and comfortable fit (see Question 158). Make adjustments, if needed, on both bands.

On the inside of the garment, press seams and darts of the garment flat. Then tack a length of 6mm (¼in) twill tape around the waistline, right on the seam line. Clip into the curve of the waistline every 1cm (⅜in) to help it fit the band – don't clip into the tape. Pin the upper band to the garment waistline, right sides together, matching notches and seams. Sew the wider or outer curve of the band to the waistline edge, not the inner curve. This is easy to get confused, because the two curves – waist and band – are in opposite directions when laid next to one another. Stitch along the tape.

Pin and sew the top edge of the under band to the top edge of the upper band, matching notches and seams. Clip curves as needed and then under stitch on the under band (see Question 121).

Turn the under band to the outside so the right sides of both bands are against each other. Stitch across the vertical ends of the waistband, clip corners and turn right side out. Finish the raw edge

of the under band with overlocking or a zigzag stitch. Turn under the finished edge and press. Hand or machine stitch in place. If you hand stitch, you can make small stitches in the waistline seam allowance that will not be visible on the right side.

ABOVE The upper band of a waistband is stitched to the waistline edge first. The under band is then stitched to the upper band.

Question 168:
There a several pieces on a curved waistband; how do I sew them together properly?

Some contoured waistbands are made of up to four pieces and because they are shaped alike, they can be easily confused as you assemble them. It is important to keep them in the proper place when sewing them together, otherwise the grain lines will not be positioned correctly, causing the band to stretch out of shape.

Separate the upper (interfaced) pieces from the lower pieces.

Some fabrics look the same on the right and wrong side, which further confuses them. When you cut them out, make sure you mark all notches on the short ends – this is key. Assemble the upper band first, then the under band. For the upper band, lay the largest piece on a flat surface, right side up. Lay the smaller pieces, right side down, on either side of the upper pieces. Match notches.

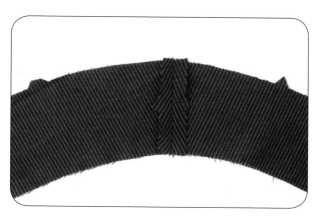

LEFT When you join together the short ends of your waistband pieces, make sure you match any notches at the seams.

Question 169:
How do I sew a bias edge waistband?

A bias edge waistband is a nice alternative to a traditional waistband. Before you attach it, verify the garment fit at the waist. Trim the waistline seam to 12mm (½in). Press darts and seams flat.

To make the waistband pattern, see Question 163. Cut a bias strip 4cm (1½in) wide and the length of the waistline plus 7.5cm (3in). This makes a finished bias edge of 12mm (½in). Pin and sew the bias strip to the waistline with a 12mm (½in) seam allowance. Leave 4cm (1½in) extending past the zip (or other closure). Press the seam allowance upward toward the strip. Sew the ends in the same manner as the straight waistband (see Question 158). Wrap the strip around the seam allowance and turn to the inside. The seam allowance remains up, not folded down to the inside. This fills out the bias strip and adds support to the waistline.

Press down and stitch in the ditch. The inside edge of the strip will not fray because it is cut on the bias. If you wish to finish the edge, though, tuck it under and hand sew.

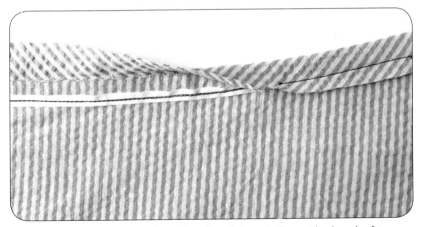

ABOVE It's a good idea to reinforce the edge of the waistline with a length of tape or stay stitching before finishing with a bias edge waistband; it helps prevent stretching.

Question 170:
How do I make a separate belt out of fabric?

A matching belt in fabric adds a nice touch to a dress or skirt and can be made easily with purchased belting or monofilament waistband stabiliser and a length of fabric.

First, cut a strip of fabric on the lengthwise grain, three times the desired width and the length of the waistline, plus 15cm (6in). Purchase the belting or monofilament in the desired width and, if you plan to add a buckle, make sure the belting fits within the buckle, plus a small amount of room for the fabric.

Fold the fabric strip in half lengthwise, to mark the centre line. Place one long edge of the belting or monofilament along the centre line of the fabric. Fold the extra width over the belting or monofilament and turn the raw edges under. Turn under the fabric at the short ends.

Edge stitch around the belt, stitching through all the layers. Press flat again. Place one end of the belt through the buckle fixture and fold it to the inside; stitch down.

ABOVE A fabric belt is easily made by folding a strip of fabric around a suitable stabiliser and stitching in place around the edges.

Question 171:
How do I make belt loops?

Belt carriers are made from a thin strip of fabric that is stitched wrong side out and then turned to the right side. The strip is then cut to shorter lengths which are sewn to the waistband at intervals.

For a standard-sized belt carrier – 12mm (½in) wide – cut a strip of fabric on the lengthwise grain about 75cm (30in) long – this length makes about five or six carriers – and 4cm (1½in) wide. (For wider carriers, cut the strip accordingly.) Fold the strip in half lengthwise, right sides together and stitch with a 6mm (¼in) seam allowance.

To turn the strip to the right side you can use a tube turner; this is a long, thin, metal tool with a small hook at one end and a loop at the other. After sewing along the fabric strip, slide the turner through the complete length of the resulting tube, hook it to the end and then pull this back up through the tube.

On a wider strip you can use a safety pin. Attach the pin to one end of the fabric strip and then push through to the other end.

Once turned to the right side, press the tube flat, with the seam on one side. Stitch two rows down the centre of the tube and cut into even lengths the width of your belt plus 12mm (½in) for ease.

ABOVE After sewing your tube of fabric you need to turn it to the right side.

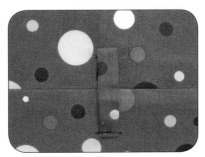

ABOVE Once you've made the belt carriers simply stitch to the garment.

10

SLEEVES

Question 172:
Set-in sleeves seem daunting; how do I begin?

A well-stitched, set-in sleeve fits comfortably and hangs accurately on the grain, with no puckering or drag lines; the seams are properly aligned where the sleeve meets the body of the garment.

The process of sewing in a sleeve begins by making sure you have accurately marked all dots and notches on your fabric pieces after cutting out the sleeves and those sections which include the armholes. You should also check that all the seam allowances (at the shoulders and sides of the bodice, and on the sleeves) have been stitched together correctly. Inaccurate seam allowances will distort the size of the armhole opening and make it difficult to insert the sleeve properly.

There are two ways to insert a sleeve. The first method is flat insertion, where the sleeve cap is sewn to the armhole before sewing the side seams and sleeve seam. The second technique is in-the-round, where the sleeve is sewn to the armhole after the side seams and sleeve seams have been stitched. The first method is a bit easier and is used mostly for shirtsleeves, T-shirts and other garments that are not close fitting. The second method is for tailored and/or more fitted garments, where the sleeve cap has a deeper curve and a more fitted sleeve.

Your pattern guide-sheet will recommend which of these methods is best for the pattern you are using. No matter which method you use, a well-stitched sleeve can be achieved with a bit of practice and patience.

Question 173:
How can I tell the right from the left sleeve when I insert them?

Although a sleeve piece looks symmetrical it does have a right and a left. The back curve differs slightly from the front so they must be sewn to the corresponding sides of the armholes. The most important step to remember is to mark the notches on the sleeve curve. A double notch indicates the back of the sleeve; a single notch is the front. If your fabric unravels easily or you are not precise when cutting, the notches often end up looking the same. The best way to avoid this mix-up is to simply leave off the front notch and only cut or mark the back notch. That way, the only notch you see on the sleeve curve will be the back

notch. This is especially important if the fabric you choose looks the same on the right and wrong sides.

EXPERT TIP

❝ As soon as you cut out the sleeves and transfer the pattern markings to the fabric, remove the tissue and pin the vertical seams, right sides together. When laid side by side, the sleeves should be mirror images of each other. This will 'set up' the sleeves as right and left and avoid confusion later on. ❞

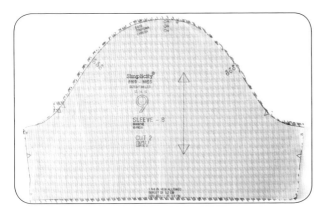

LEFT When cutting out sleeves from two layers of fabric, remember to keep the fabric wrong or right sides together so the sleeves are not identical, but mirror images of each other.

Question 174:
How do I avoid puckers when I sew a set-in sleeve?

This is probably the most important part of sewing in sleeves. Because the curve of a sleeve is bigger (by up to 4cm (1½in)) than the armhole into which it is being sewn, it must be made to fit. This is done with ease stitching worked around to the sleeve cap, which is then drawn up to fit the sleeve into the armhole.

The first step is to sew two rows of tacking around the cap between the notches (or 5cm (2in) from each end of the curve). Make sure they are parallel, with one row exactly on the seam (1.5cm (⅝in) for most patterns) and the other 6mm (¼in) beside it, toward the raw edge. Leave thread tails on both rows. Pull the top thread of each row at the same time to draw up the sleeve slightly. Move the gathers around the sleeve cap, with most of them near the top of the curve.

Pin first at the shoulder seam, matching the dot that marks the centre top of the sleeve curve to the shoulder seam. Work with the sleeve side up and use lots of pins, as needed. Be sure the raw edges line up – it's easy to slide them around, but they must be lined up for correct fit and alignment of the seam. Continue to move the gathers around the curve, just enough for the ripples to stay on the seam allowance side of the tacking. Tack in place and check for puckers before machine stitching.

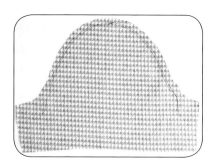

ABOVE Use two rows of machine tacking to draw up the sleeve cap.

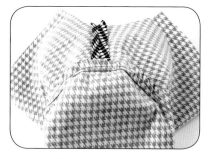

ABOVE After pinning the sleeve cap into the armhole, stitch in place.

Question 175:
How do I sew gathered sleeves?

A gathered sleeve, sometimes called a puff sleeve, is a variation of a set-in sleeve, but in this case, you don't have to worry about avoiding puckers, because the gathers (or puckers) are the chief feature of the design of this sleeve. Because of this, it's a much easier type of sleeve to insert. The sleeve cap on a puff sleeve is fuller and wider, and requires noticeable gathers to fit it into the armhole.

To prepare the sleeve, stitch two rows of machine tacked stitches around the curve, stopping 5cm (2in) from either end. Pin and gather the sleeve as described in Question 174, but as you pin, distribute the gathers evenly. Make sure there are no gathers on the garment side of the seam but only on the sleeve side. Stitch the sleeve at normal stitch length. To reduce bulk in the sleeve (with all those gathers), trim the seam between sleeve and bodice, and zigzag the edge, or stitch down with an overlocker.

Check the seam on the right side before finishing the seam edge. Look at both sleeves and make sure the gathers look evenly distributed, and the profile of the 'puff' is the same on both sleeves.

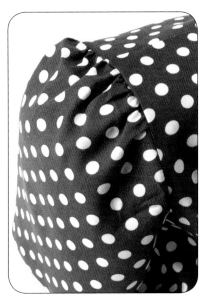

ABOVE A 'puff' sleeve makes a feature of the gathers which are created when fitting the sleeve into the armhole.

Question 176:
My sleeve hangs crooked; what should I do?

If, after making your test garment, your set-in sleeve looks crooked when you stand sideways in front of the mirror, it may have to be reinserted correctly. To find the correct placement, remove the sleeve from the garment and then try on the garment again and place the sleeve on your arm separately. Pin the sleeve in place at the top and rotate it until it looks and feels comfortable. (You may find it useful to get help with this task.)

Remove the garment and on the inside, pin the seam as it will be sewn, right along the stitch line. Try on the garment again (watching out for pins!) and check the results. Continue to adjust until the sleeve hangs vertically, which means the grain line is vertical as it should be. This adjustment is sometimes needed because the dot on the sleeve pattern was not marked and placed at the shoulder line, or if your shoulders tend to roll or tilt forward. Your personal shoulder position changes the way the sleeves hang and so the garment must be adjusted accordingly.

Question 177:
Can I eliminate the sleeves?

If your pattern does not include a sleeveless option, it is possible to convert the garment to a sleeveless style easily. The best option is to replace the sleeve with a facing finish for the armhole.

Before you create the facing, however, try on the test garment (in case you need to alter the pattern) and check the position of the underarm at the seam line. If it's too high, lower the armhole curve just a bit (see Question 43). If your bra shows, go back to the tissue pattern and raise the underarm curve as described in Question 44.

Once the fit is verified, make patterns for the armhole facing.

EXPERT TIP

66 You can also sew the facing to the armhole before stitching the side seams of the garment and facings. Lay the garment flat (shoulder seams are stitched front to back) and sew the facing on. After you clip and under stitch the seam, match the underarm (or side) seam of both the facing and the garment, and sew the side seams all at once. Turn the facing to the inside and press. **99**

Trace over the front pattern piece, tracing along the shoulder line, around the armhole and along the side seam for about 7.5cm (3in). Then draw in a curved line about 7.5cm (3in) from the armhole curve. Cut out the shape created to make the front facing pattern. The area you are tracing will probably not include the grain line, so you will need to work out where it is in relation to the armhole and draw it on to your pattern. Repeat on the back pattern piece. Alternatively, photocopy your pattern pieces and then draw in a new line, 7.5cm (3in) from the armhole curves to mark the pattern edge.

Use your patterns to cut two front and two back facing pieces, as well as the corresponding number of interfacing pieces. Fuse the interfacing to the facing pieces and then stitch the facing pieces together at the shoulder and side seams. Stay stitch the curved armhole edges on both the facing

and the garment. Pin the facings to the garment armholes, right sides together, and stitch, as described in Question 82. Clip the seam (see Question 83) and turn the facing to the inside of the garment; press.

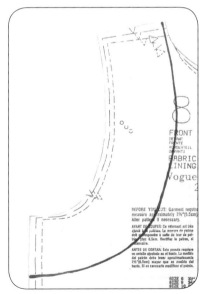

ABOVE If you photocopy your front and back patterns you can draw on them to create a facing pattern.

Question 178:
How do I sew a simple placket?

A placket is an opening at the wrist of a cuffed sleeve that has a button closure. It is positioned so it faces backwards and towards the body when the garment is worn. The placket is created when the sleeve is cut from the wrist into the sleeve. The raw edge of this cut is then covered with a strip of fabric sewn to the edge.

To sew the placket, cut a strip of fabric on the grain that is twice the length of the slit and 2.5cm (1in) wide. Sew one long edge of the strip to the slit, right sides together,

taking a 6mm (¼in) seam allowance. Press the seam allowance away from the slit, or outwards. Wrap the other edge of the strip around the seam allowance and fold to the inside. Line the fold up with the first row of stitching and pin in place. Stitch down along the fold. Press flat. Bring the placket ends together at the wrist edge, folding one to the inside so it lays over the other side. This forms a corner at the top of the slit on the underside. Sew diagonally across the corner to hold the placket in place.

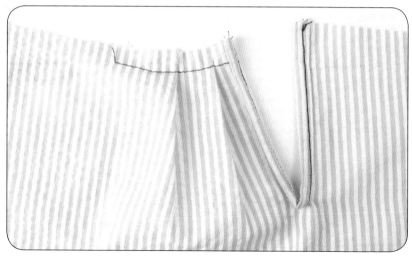

ABOVE The placket is formed at the wrist by cutting a slit into the sleeve and edging it with a narrow strip of matching fabric, cut on the grain.

Question 179:
How do I sew a cuff to a sleeve?

A cuff is a separate piece of fabric sewn to the end of a sleeve, usually on a long sleeve shirt or blouse. The most common type of cuff has a button closure to secure the opening and a placket (see Question 178) to allow the hand to get in and out of it comfortably.

Before you sew the cuff to the sleeve, assemble the cuff and turn it right side out. The pleats and placket of the sleeve must also be stitched and pressed in place before attaching the cuff. To sew on the cuff, pin the interfaced layer only, to the wrist, right sides together, matching notches. If the sleeve is gathered instead of pleated, sew two rows of tacking and ease the fabric at the wrist edge into the cuff edge. Stitch and press the seam toward the cuff. Turn under the raw edge of the other layer of the cuff so the fold lines up with the seam. Machine stitch down or hand sew the cuff edge.

ABOVE Finish off sewing a cuff to a sleeve by turning under the last raw edge and hand stitching all round.

Question 180:
How do I add a turned-up cuff?

This addition must be decided on at the fabric-cutting stage so you have enough extra at the bottom edge of the sleeve to form the cuff. This works only on a sleeve that is straight and not tapered at the wrist. Determine the finished length of the sleeve and add double the cuff width plus 2.5cm (1in) – for a 5cm (2in) deep cuff, add 12.5cm (5in) to the sleeve hem. Make sure you've stitched up the sleeve seam.

Fold the sleeve hem under by the finished width of the cuff plus 2.5cm (1in); so for a 5cm (2in) deep cuff, fold under by 7.5cm (3in). Press and sew the hem close to the raw edge. Turn up the finished hem to the outside to form the finished

cuff. Press flat, making sure both cuffs are the same width. Stitch the cuff down at the underarm seam.

ABOVE A turned-up cuff is a smart way to finish tailored sleeves at the wrist.

Question 181:
Are there decorative ways to finish a sleeve at the wrist?

You can add a creative touch to the edge of your sleeve in several ways, other than the various types of cuffs. One option is to finish the sleeve with elastic and a small

ruffle. Decide on how deep you want the ruffle and measure the width of the elastic (a good width is a 2cm (¾in) ruffle and 12mm (½in) elastic); add these two together and add on 1.5cm (⅝in) for the seam allowance. Make sure you add on this amount to the end of the sleeve as hem allowance when you come to cut out the sleeve.

Finish the raw edge at the wrist and then turn under the hem by the hem allowance you've calculated; press in place. Stitch around the hem at the depth you want the ruffle. Then stitch round the hem again, the width of the elastic from the first line of stitching; leave a gap in this stitching so you can insert the elastic. To measure the elastic length, wrap it round your hand. Using a bodkin, thread the elastic through the casing at the wrist, then sew the elastic ends together. Stitch the opening closed.

You can also finish a sleeve with a bias trim. Sew a bias binding strip to the hem edge, cut from the same or a contrasting fabric. Cut the bias strip 2.5cm (1in) wide and long enough to wrap around your hand (there is very little room to stretch or give, unlike elastic). Sew tacking stitches at the edge of the sleeve and gather up to fit to the length of the bias binding. Pin and sew one edge of the binding to the sleeve, adjusting gathers as you go. Press the seam toward the binding. Turn the other edge of the binding to the inside. Fold again to cover the seam allowance and stitch down.

Both of these methods should be sewn after the underarm seam of the sleeve has been stitched to reduce bulk and create a smoother look to the finished sleeve.

ABOVE You can finish a sleeve at the wrist with an elasticated and ruffled hem (left), or with a bias trim (right).

Question 182:
How do I hem or finish a cuffless sleeve?

A sleeve without a cuff can be finished with a simple hem. A short sleeve looks best with a 2.5cm (1in) deep hem; a long sleeve can have a hem up to 4cm (1½in) deep.

First finish the raw edge of the sleeve at the wrist; this can be done with zigzag stitch or with an overlocker, or you can turn under the edge by 6mm (¼in) and in and press in place. Then turn under the hem edge by the required amount and pin in place; make sure the hem is the same depth all round. Press and then stitch the hem in place, either by machine or by hand.

If your sleeves taper towards the end, the sewing pattern should flare out at the wrist, so that you have enough fabric at the hem to turn it under neatly.

Question 183:
What is a raglan sleeve and how do I assemble one?

Raglan sleeves, unlike set-in sleeves, are joined to the garment with a seam that starts at the underarm and slants upward to meet the side front and back of the neckline. They are often found in jackets, coats and T-shirts. Raglan sleeves are easy to insert because there is no ease stitching or gathering required.

The assembly process for a garment with raglan sleeves is a bit different than those with set-in sleeves. The sleeves are sewn to the main garment pieces before the side seam and underarm seams are stitched. Darts are used to shape the sleeve so it fits well around the shoulder and upper arm, or the sleeve may be made up of two or more parts and so features seams that extend from top to bottom (or neckline to wrist).

Question 184:
How do I make a cap sleeve?

A cap sleeve is formed by simply extending a garment at the shoulder seam so that it hangs just beyond the edge of the wearer's shoulder. You can add the cap after you have pinned the garment pattern pieces to your fabric but before you have cut it out.

Pin the front bodice piece to your chosen fabric. With a thin chalk marker, draw a line on the fabric that extends the shoulder line by 2.5–7.5cm (1–3in). Redraw the armhole curve starting at the underarm and curving upward to meet the new end point of the shoulder seam. Repeat on the back bodice piece, extending the shoulder seam by exactly the same amount as on the front.

It's a good idea to make up a test garment to ensure the look and fit of your alteration. Sew the shoulder seams as directed in your pattern guide sheet. Instead of a facing around the armhole though, stitch a narrow hem by machine or by hand.

ABOVE A cap sleeve works well in a loose-fitting garment made from a soft, lightweight fabric.

11
CLOSURES AND TRIMS

Question 185:
What type of closures are available?

Closures are what holds a garment in place while it is being worn – such as the zip in a fly front, or the buttons on a coat. Some clothes require no closures at all – skirts with elasticated waists, for example, or wrap-round dresses and coats. Most garments, however, require some kind of closure and there are many types from which to choose.

Closures are either visible or invisible. Among the visible closures are certain zips, buttons (with buttonholes or loop fastenings), toggles (also known as frogs), and certain larger hooks and eyes. Some visible closures are used to add a decorative element to a garment and some may even have no practical purpose at all. Smaller closures such as press studs, and hooks and eyes, are usually hidden, and there are ways of concealing zips so they become virtually invisible.

Most patterns will suggest what type of closure to use on your garment, but since there are several options, you can choose which ones work best with the style of the garment, or just choose what you think will add to the style and creativity of the finished item.

Closure	Suitable for...
Standard zip – centred	Centre-front or centre-back of skirts, dresses and tops.
Standard zip – lapped	Side and back seam openings in skirts, dresses and trousers.
Separating zip	Front openings on jackets and coats; any seam opening that is open at both ends.
Invisible zip	Front, back and side openings in skirts, dresses and trousers.
Buttons – with buttonholes	Front openings in coats, jackets, blouses and shirts; at cuffs; to secure neck openings and waistbands.
Buttons – with loops	At neck openings and cuffs; any garment that makes a feature of many small buttons, such as wedding gowns and evening wear.
Toggles/frogs	Used for coats and jackets, where the fastening is a particular feature.
Press studs	At the top of zip fastenings, to secure neck openings and waistbands; on any overlapping opening where the closure should be invisible.
Hooks and eyes	As for press studs, but also used on abutting openings. Can be used for front openings in certain coats, jackets, blouses and shirts instead of buttons.

Question 186:
How do I decide what type of zip to use?

There are several types of insertion methods for zips and deciding which one to use will likely depend on your skill level, what type of zip you have available at the time, and what method is best suited for your garment. In other words, you have many options.

The types of zips available for purchase include: standard or regular, separating and invisible. However, there are several ways to insert them. A standard zip is most often inserted by either the centred or lapped method, and these methods work well in dresses and skirts. A separating zip is usually inserted in a jacket that opens completely along the centre front of the garment. An invisible zip is often found in better quality dresses and skirts.

Whatever zip type you choose and method of insertion you use, the process is easier if you have a zip foot attachment for your sewing machine. This attachment is usually part of the basic accessory kit that comes with your machine. The exception to this is an invisible zip attachment, which can be purchased separately. While it is possible to insert this type of zip with the zip foot that comes with your machine, it will be easier and the result will be much better if you use the special attachment designed for an invisible zip.

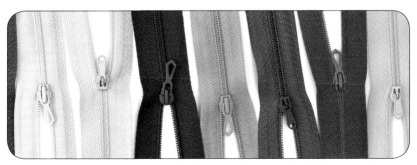

ABOVE Zips come in a wide range of different shades, so it should be no trouble to find one to match your chosen fabric.

Question 187:
How do I sew a lapped zip?

A lapped zip has one row of stitches showing on the outside of the garment. It uses an all-purpose zip and is commonly inserted in side and back seams. To prepare the seam for the zip, tack the seam for the length of the zip, and then sew with a normal stitch length for the rest of the seam. Press the seam open and lay it seam-side up on a flat surface.

HERE'S HOW

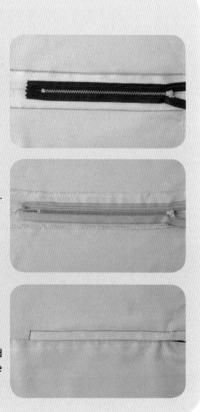

- Place the zip, right side down, over the pressed-open seam, making sure the teeth are centred on the seam. Pin the zip tape to one side of the seam allowance only. With a zip foot fitted, machine tack the left-hand side of the zip tape to the seam allowance; do not catch the garment in the stitching. Close the zip (top).
- Turn the zip face up and leave other layers as they are, to the left. A fold forms between the teeth and the seam. Push this so it rests next to the teeth; stitch the fold down, right next to the teeth (centre).
- Turn garment to right side and sew through all layers to stitch down the right-hand side of the zip tape. Begin with needle placed in the seam, 12mm (½in) below the bottom stop. Sew across the zip for 12mm (½in), then to the top of the zip (bottom).
- Remove the tacking stitches that held the seam in place to access the zip. The lap should be on the left of the seam when seen from right side.

Question 188:
How do I sew an invisible zip?

An invisible zip differs from other zips because it is sewn to an open seam. A special foot is available and the zip must be an invisible type. An invisible-zip foot has two grooves on the underside which fit the coils, left and right, when the presser foot is down, allowing you to sew close to the coils without stitching over them. If you don't have an invisible foot, use a standard zip foot and sew close to the coils, holding the coils flat as you sew.

HERE'S HOW

• First mark the seam line on the garment front, at the zip opening; use chalk or a line of tacking. Open the zip and place the left zip tape, right side down, on the seam line of the left-hand garment piece. Position the zip coils so they run along the marked seam line; pin.

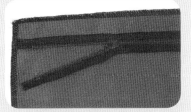

• Using an invisible-zip foot, stitch from top to bottom, stopping when you get to the zip pull (top). Check to see if the zip closes and opens freely. If not, you may have stitched on the coil. If so, remove the stitches and restitch.

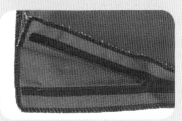

• Pin the other side of the zip tape to the other seam allowance, lining it up as before. Stitch as for the left-hand side of the zip (centre).

• Close the zip and turn the garment over to right side; press gently. Apart from the zip pull, the zip is virtually invisible (bottom).

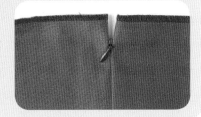

Question 189:
My zip is too long; can I shorten it?

Sometimes the length and colour of zip you need is not available. If you must choose one over the other, go with the right colour, because it is possible to shorten a zip. (It's always better to buy a zip that is too long rather than shorter than that required by the pattern guide.)

To shorten a zip, make a new bottom stop and cut off the old one. Determine the correct length you need, plus 2.5cm (1in), and stitch several small stitches across the teeth. Sew carefully so you don't break the machine needle. Then cut off the rest of the zip 12mm (½in) beyond the new stop. This works for all-purpose and invisible polyester and nylon zips with teeth that are small to medium size.

For separating zips and all-purpose metal zips, you must cut off from the top because you need the closure intact on a separating zip. For a metal zip, you must also cut off at the top, because you cannot sew across the bottom of the metal. Cut off the top only after it has been completely sewn into the garment and while the zip is open. Before you cut, place a safety pin on both sides at the top to keep the slider from falling off once you cut the top stops off.

ABOVE Stitching several times across the bottom of an over-long zip will effectively create a new 'stop'. Cut off the unwanted excess zip below this point.

Question 190:
How do I determine where to place buttons and buttonholes?

Sewing on buttons and making buttonholes is the final step to completing your garment. While pattern pieces do provide markings for button placement, it's often better to decide on position yourself during the final fitting.

Since buttonholes are stitched before the buttons are sewn in place, mark their location before marking the placement of the buttons (see Question 192).

EXPERT TIP
66 **If your buttons are small, consider sewing the buttonholes in sets of twos to add interest to the closure.** 99

For a centre front closure with horizontal buttonholes, try on the garment and pin it closed. In women's clothing, the right-hand sidea of a closure overlaps the left. Mark the line where the right-hand side overlaps the left. That way, each time you try on the garment, you know the exact placement of each side of the garment.

Using a pin, mark the position of the first buttonhole; this should be right at the bust line. Remove the garment and with a seam gauge, pin mark the remaining buttonhole positions according to the distance you have decided – 7.5cm (3in) apart is a good amount. The top button may be above the button at the bust line. Before sewing the buttonholes, mark the stop and start of each one with two rows of chalk.

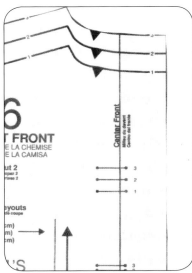

ABOVE Sewing patterns often indicate the placement of buttonholes.

Question 191:
How do I sew a buttonhole?

Buttonholes can be stitched by machine or by hand. Most sewing machines have a buttonhole option and your owner's manual will provide you with full instructions. If, however, your model does not feature this function or if your garment is too thick to go into your sewing machine, you can try a hand-sewn buttonhole.

To determine the correct buttonhole size, use a seam gauge to measure the diameter of one button. Then measure the thickness and multiply by two. Add this to the button diameter; this is the length of your buttonhole. Make all your machine-sewn buttonholes at the same time and work from top to bottom. When you've finished, tie off the ends by pulling the thread tails to the inside. To cut the buttonholes, use a seam ripper to slice through the fabric between the rows of stitching.

To sew a buttonhole by hand, first hand or machine stitch a rectangle shape around your marked buttonhole. Use a seam ripper to cut along the marking, keeping the slit inside the stitching. Thread your needle with a thick thread and secure on the wrong side at one end of the slit. Bring the needle through the slit. Insert the needle in the fabric, from right side to wrong side, just outside your first line of stitching; push the needle tip back through the slit but don't pull it through. Loop the thread behind the needle tip, then pull the needle through. Continue in this way all round the buttonhole, until all the raw edges are concealed.

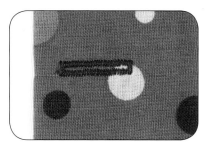

ABOVE Cut the slits in machine-made buttonholes after stitching.

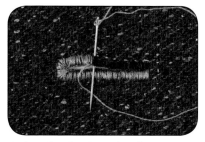

ABOVE Cut the slits in hand-sewn buttonholes before stitching.

Question 192:
How do I sew on a button?

Buttons are sewn on after the buttonholes have been stitched and cut. To get them in the right position, lie the garment flat and pin the closure in place, with buttonhole side overlapping. Starting at the top, push a chalk pencil through the buttonhole to make a mark underneath. Mark just the first button.

Use a double strand of thread and secure it on the wrong side. For a hole-type button, hold it in place with one hand, and bring the needle up through the fabric and the first hole of the button. Insert the needle through the next hole and

ABOVE Push a chalk pencil through a buttonhole to mark the button position.

EXPERT TIP

❝ If a button is heavy, it may sag a bit on the garment. To avoid this, sew the shank down twice on either side close to the button and place it so the shank is vertical on the garment. ❞

back down through the fabric. After the first stitch, slide a toothpick between the stitches and the button and leave it there. Before the final stitch, remove the toothpick and then wrap the thread around the stitches under the button to raise it above the fabric.

If you are stitching on a shank button (one with a loop underneath), there is no need to create extra slack as you stitch the button in place. Simply stitch neatly through the button shank until the button feels securely attached.

Once you've stitched on the first button, push it through the first buttonhole and then mark the position of the second buttonhole as before and then sew on the second button. Continue in this way until all the buttons are attached.

Question 193:
How do I make button loops?

Button loops are hand sewn as a substitute for a traditional buttonhole or other type of closure. To sew a button loop, first cut a long length of thread – about 50cm (20in) – and thread your needle. Pull the thread through until the ends are even and tie in a knot, so you have a double thickness of thread.

Secure the thread on the wrong side of the fabric and then bring the needle through to the right side at the point where you want the button loop to start. Insert the needle back through the fabric, roughly the button's diameter away from where the thread emerged. Draw the thread through but not all the way – leave a loop of thread on the surface that's long enough to fit over the button.

Bring the needle back out on the right side as close to the same point as possible and then insert it again at the other end of the loop. Pull the thread through until it matches the first loop. Repeat this once more until you have a loop made up of six strands of thread.

Bring the needle to the right side at the base of the loop. Bring the needle under the loop, from right to left, and over the thread, so that you make a knot on the loop. Pull the knot down the loop so it sits snug on the fabric before pulling it tight. Repeat to make the next knot, making sure this one sits snug against the first knot. Continue until you have covered the thread loops; draw the needle through to the wrong side and tie off securely.

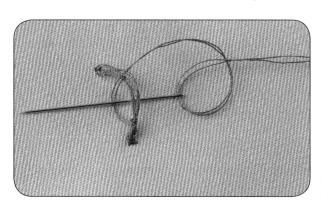

LEFT Button loops are made by covering loops of thread with a series of tight knots.

Question 194:
What are hook and eyes, and where should they be used?

Hook and eyes are a favourite type of closure, most often found at the top of an opening in a dress, skirt or trousers. They can be used as a stand-alone closure or alongside a zip or buttons for additional support. They come in a variety of sizes and can be purchased in various colours – silver (nickel), black or white. You can also find particularly large sized hooks and eyes, sometimes covered in fabric, for use with heavier fabrics, such as when making a coat. It's a good idea to have a few different sizes of hooks and eyes amongst your store of sewing notions.

The hook side of this type of closure has two metal loops or holes at the base of the hook shape that are sewn down. The other side, the eye, also has two loops that are sewn down, with a larger metal loop or a straight piece that sits between the smaller loops. If being used on an overlapping opening, the hook is, generally speaking, sewn to the overlap; the eye on the underlap.

ABOVE Hooks and eyes are small but significant closures.

Question 195:
How do I attach hook and eyes?

Hooks and eyes are stitched in place by hand. Start by closing the opening in the garment as you would like it look when worn; this can be zipped, buttoned or even pinned in place. Use a chalk pencil to mark the position of the hook. Thread your needle and secure the thread at the marked position; make sure this is not visible on the right side of the garment. Hold the hook in place with one hand and bring the needle up through the fabric and one of the metal loops at the base of the hook. Make one small stitch to secure this loop, then make another small stitch to secure the adjacent loop and hold the hook in place. Go back to the first loop and make small stitches all round; repeat to stitch down the second loop and secure the hook.

To stitch on the eye, first loop it over the hook and then hold in place against the fabric. Make a small stitch in both of the loops at the base of the eye, to hold it in place. Unhook the hook and then continue to make small stitches through the eye's loops to secure.

If you are sewing at the top of a zip, the garment edges above the zip should touch. Also, sew onto the inner layers only, so the stitches don't show on the right side.

EXPERT TIP

66 **For extra security when stitching hooks and eyes in place, thread your needle with a doubled length of thread.** 99

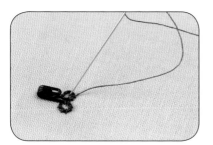

ABOVE Secure the loops at the base of the hook with small even stitches.

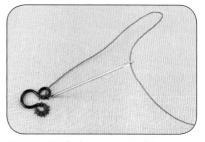

ABOVE Stitch the eye part of the closure in a similar way.

Question 196:
What are press studs and where should I use them?

Another popular closure, press studs are used at an opening where edges overlap — at the the the centre front of a garment, for example — in place of buttons. Because press studs are small, they work best in areas with minimal strain. Like hooks and eyes, press studs come in a variety of sizes and colours — silver (nickel), black and white. You can also get clear press studs, which are particularly useful for lightweight fabrics, especially sheers. Generally speaking, press studs are sewn on in such a way as to be invisible, but they can be used as a decorative feature and you can even cover them for an especially unique look.

Press studs are made up of two parts. One half is the ball part; the other is the socket part. The ball is pushed into the socket to make the press stud close. If you look closely at the ball part you will see a small hole in the tip of the ball. Inserting a needle or pin through this hole helps correctly position the press stud (see Question 197). There are holes around the rim of each part of a press stud; they are sewn in place through these holes. When placed against the fabric, they should lay flat. Generally speaking, the ball part is sewn to the overlap; the socket part to the underlap.

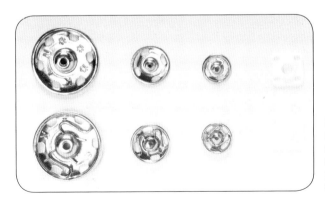

LEFT Press studs, also known as snaps, have two sections — the ball part presses into the socket part.

Question 197:
How do I sew on press studs?

To sew on a press stud, first you need to determine the correct position. Hold or pin the garment opening in place and use chalk to mark where you want the ball part to be. Push a pin through the fabric at this mark so that the point of the pin is on the side to which you are sewing the press stud. Slip the hole in the ball part onto the pin's tip and slide it down until it lies flat on the fabric. Make a small stitch through each hole in the press stud to secure and then remove the pin. Continue to sew the press stud in place, making three or four small stitches at each hole.

To mark the socket position, rub chalk on the ball and press it against the fabric on other side of the opening. Hold the socket part down onto the fabric with a finger while you stitch it in place in the same way as for the ball part.

Covered press studs are easily hidden and add a couture touch to a garment. To cover, cut a circle of fabric (lining fabric is less bulky) and tack around the circumference. Place the socket part of the press stud, right side down, in the middle of the circle. Snap it together with the ball part to spread the fabric into the socket. Make sure it snaps correctly and draw up the tacking stitches. Stitch the fabric down to secure the press stud.

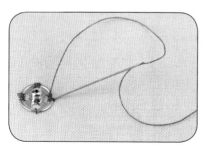

ABOVE Make small stitches in the holes around the ball section to secure.

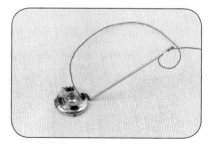

ABOVE Stitch down the socket section in a similar way.

Question 198:
Where should I add a trim?

Trims are a wonderful way to enhance a garment design. The list of options seems endless, but includes braid, rick-rack, fringing, lace, embroidered bands and ribbon. You can be as creative as you wish, but keep in mind that any trim you add should complement your design rather than compete with its other aspects or overwhelm the finish item. The weight, width and style of your intended trim should match the garment. A simple trim against an elaborate design or fabric can bring focus to the overall design, whereas an elaborate trim on a dress with simple lines can add just the right amount of interest to make the garment really stand out.

The most obvious place to add trim is around the outer edges of a garment, such as at the neckline, the hem or sleeve edge. But you could also consider adding a trimming to the significant positions within a garment – such as on the collar, across the top of a pocket, at the yoke seam or along the seam of empire waistline.

The possibilities are endless and so are the various trims. If you can't find what you want in the fabric notions department, venture into upholstery and home décor where many textures, colours and sizes abound. Adding trims is also a great way to update an existing garment.

Question 199:
How do I apply trim to straight and curved edges?

Some trims must be sewn in place during the construction process and others can be added when the garment is completed. For example, a lace trim or embroidery band may need to be sewn to the neckline before you attach the facing. Other trims, such as beading, lace or rick-rack, can be sewn on after a garment is completed. The advantage to these is that you can experiment with how they will look and change easily if needed.

When you sew the trim, start and end it in an inconspicuous place, like at a cross seam, or a side seam. Check to see that the care instructions of the trim matches the

care instructions of the rest of the garment fabric.

Be mindful that a straight trim – that is, one which does not bend or curve easily when laid flat, may not fit well on a curved edge. Depending on how maleable the trim is, you may be able to manipulate its shape as you sew it down by hand. The trim should lay flat and smooth against the garment. If you are not sure how the decoration will work with the garment, tack it in place and try the garment on to be sure the trim lays flat and doesn't distort the garment. For instance, a beaded trim on a neckline may cause drooping if it is too heavy.

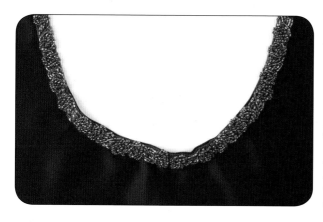

LEFT When trimming a scooped neckline you need to pick a decorative element that will curve when stitched in place.

Question 200:
How do I make my own bias trim?

To make the bias trim, decide on the finished width needed and cut strips of fabric on a precise 45 degree angle to the lengthwise or crosswise grains (see Question 49). The width should be the desired finished width plus 2.5cm (1in) for 12mm (½in) turnings. To join multiple lengths, cut each strip end at a diagonal to the bias, which means the cut end is on a straight grain. Sew the ends, right sides together, with an overlap of 6mm (¼in).

To fold under the edges of the bias tape, use a bias tape maker – they come in different sizes. At the ironing board, slide the strip, right side down, into the wide end of the tape maker. Use a pin to pull the fabric along until it appears at the other end. Position the tip of the iron at the narrow end and press

EXPERT TIP

66 Unlike adding a bias strip to create a facing or edge, bias trim is turned, pressed and finished before it is stitched to the garment. 99

the tape folds down as you pull the tape maker along the strip. Trim the corners of cross seams, since they may not fit into the tape maker.

Once you have your strip pressed, it is ready to add to your garment. It can be topstitched down like a trim, or it can be used as a binding on a neckline or any raw edge. You may wish to adhere the strip first with fusible web, then topstitch in place.

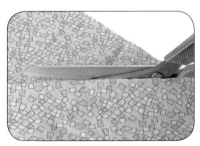

ABOVE Cut strips of fabric at 45 degrees to the length- or crosswise grain.

ABOVE Draw the strips through a tape maker to turn under the edges.

Index

Page numbers in **bold** refer to illustrations

Acknowledgements

All illustrations are copyright Quantum Publishing (Marcos Bevilacqua) with the following exceptions:

front cover (main) Shutterstock/Diego Cervo; front cover (bottom, from left to right) Shutterstock/nito, Shutterstock/gnohz, Shutterstock/krugloff, Shutterstock/Ewa Walicka, Shutterstock/Pincasso; 2 Shutterstock/Alenavlad; 9 Shutterstock/AVAVA; 10 Shutterstock/Africa Studio; 23 Shutterstock/Inga Ivanova; 25 Shutterstock/PeJo; 31 Quantum Publishing (Caroline Dear); 32–36, 38–41, 43–46 & 48–51 Quantum Publishing (David Jones); 53 Shutterstock/ krugloff; 54 Shutterstock/hxdbzxy; 75 Shutterstock/Zhukov Oleg; 91 Shutterstock/jupeart; 119 Shutterstock/John Kershner; 126 Shutterstock/Henrik Winther Andersen; 133, 151, 152, 163, 175 Shutterstock/Karkas; 191 Shutterstock/Africa Studio; 205 Getty Images/Steve Allen; 207 Shutterstock/nito; 215 Shutterstock/Pinkcandy; 217 Getty Images/Peter Anderson; back cover Shutterstock/Siberian Lena.

Useful Contacts and Resources

www.marymccarthysews.com

www.burdastyle.com/patterns
http://butterick.mccall.com
http://mccallpattern.mccall.com
www.simplicity.com
http://voguepatterns.mccall.com

www.nancysnotions.com
www.sewessential.co.uk

www.asg.org
www.isew.co.uk
www.startsewing.co.uk
www.sewing.org